ENGLISH INSTITUTIONS

General Editor:
LORD STAMP

E. T. CRUTCHLEY
C.B., C.M.G., C.B.E.

G P O

CAMBRIDGE
AT THE UNIVERSITY PRESS
1938

CAMBRIDGE
UNIVERSITY PRESS

University Printing House, Cambridge CB2 8BS, United Kingdom

Cambridge University Press is part of the University of Cambridge.

It furthers the University's mission by disseminating knowledge in the pursuit of
education, learning and research at the highest international levels of excellence.

www.cambridge.org
Information on this title: www.cambridge.org/9781107511644

© Cambridge University Press 1938

First published 1938
First paperback edition 2015

A catalogue record for this publication is available from the British Library

ISBN 978-1-107-51164-4 Paperback

GENERAL EDITOR'S PREFACE

A series of new books on English Institutions may seem, on the one hand, to run a grave risk of duplicating or overlapping many existing volumes, or of dealing only with the trivial on the other. The development of the more important and prominent has had many chroniclers, for in the nature of things and by their fitness for their essential functions, they must have a great deal in common with similar Institutions abroad and little that is distinctive for treatment in a national sense. The unique ones would be those that serve less universal purposes and that, therefore, find themselves in a secondary rank. The opening volume of this series, however, dispels these misconceptions and belies these prejudgments. Nothing could be more universal than the functions of a State Post Office; nothing could be more distinctive than the British leadership in this development or than the present position held by this national Institution. Mr Crutchley has written a book which is entirely original and, within my knowledge, duplicates no other; even familiar matter has been presented in a new setting, and the whole treatment is sound and functional in its historical leads, and impressively informative in its description of the Institution as it is to-day.

Man's life in modern society, however individualistic, increasingly expresses itself through Institutions, and his life in any land can only be described and understood by his participation in them and his loyalty to them. The conventional description of the activities of a particular individual dips into Institutions widely, here and there, touching all the types and uses of groups, from point to point, in turn. It is a useful complementary method to describe and to account for each of the Institutions in itself and as a whole, as impersonally and generally as possible, subordinating the personal view or the isolated service. In this way a composite picture of society may be constructed which describes not so much how an Englishman lives, as the *means* by which he lives and expresses himself.

It is confidently anticipated that this series will provide new emphasis, and explain many neglected but important phases in our national life. Even the most deeply rooted and long established of our Institutions has to make new alignments of its purposes, and modifications of its methods, to meet the totally different mental attitude of this generation and to accommodate the "pace of change", if it is to serve the present age and also to survive. This then, after a severe period of adjustment, is a peculiarly suitable time at which to take stock of the present situation and aims, and their true place in our corporate and personal life. Mr Crutchley has a great story to tell and he has told it worthily, with inside knowledge and a departmental pride, in leash, which is the surest warrant of attractive presentation.

STAMP

CONTENTS

ILLUSTRATIONS

Photographs by G.P.O. Public Relations Department

Dedicated to

SIR THOMAS ROBERT GARDINER
K.C.B., K.B.E.
Director General of the Post Office

<hr>
<hr>

PREFACE

Returning to the service of the Post Office in 1935 after
an absence of twenty-one years, I was struck at once by
two facts. The first was the dramatic development which
had taken place in all departments since the pre-war days,
and especially the immense acceleration of that development which is a feature of the present decade. I have
attempted to indicate this rapid progress in the impression—it is no more than an impression—of the various
services contained in this book.

The second fact that struck me was the intense pride in
the service shown by all who had a hand in its administration and operation. In this there was nothing new. Post
Office people have always been intensely proud of their
own special bit of the great machine, and quietly appreciative of the other bits, and of the machine as a whole.

But I mention the matter here because I have traded upon it quite shamelessly in compiling these pages.

For the help I have thus received from numerous colleagues in many departments and grades of the service I offer my sincere thanks. I also acknowledge my debt to the several authors of books and pamphlets on the Post Office and its various services which I have drawn upon for information, and here I should be at fault if I omitted special mention of the work on the Post Office written some twelve years ago by Sir Evelyn Murray, K.C.B., the last to hold the post of "Secretary".

It is customary to talk of the "new" Post Office which is supposed to have come into being as a result of agitations and inquests culminating in the year 1932. Changes there undoubtedly were at that time, changes in administration and changes in practice, but it must always be remembered that the strides which the Post Office has made in recent years have been possible only because of the firm track laid by Sir Evelyn Murray and his colleagues, often in very discouraging circumstances, in years gone by.

E. T. C.

October 1938

CHAPTER 1

THE MACHINE IN
ACTION

There can surely be very few people in the country to-day
who are not to some degree dependent on Post Office
services. Yet to the vast majority, the Post Office is only
known by its postmen, by the men and women at the
counters, by the telegraph messengers and, rather more
vaguely, by an occasional red mail van, a vista of poles
carrying wires, a man wheeling a truck of mail bags along
a busy railway platform, or a black tarpaulin shelter
covering a hole in the pavement, the access to unknown
wire systems and undreamt-of complications. All the rest
of the paraphernalia, the throbbing activity behind the
scenes, is, or was, taken for granted. But a mechanical-
minded generation has sprung up, and with it a growing
desire to see how this mighty machine works.

The Post Office, to tell the truth, has of recent years
pandered to this desire. The atmosphere of mystery in
which it formerly worked, like every other Government
department, was suddenly dissipated. The public was no
longer told to keep its distance, but was invited to come
behind and look around. Post Office literature shed its
gloomy blue covers and its forbidding phraseology and
burst into colours and ordinary colloquial English. The
post offices themselves took on a brighter look. Dingy
fittings assumed an attractive bronze, the litter of notices

and placards was gradually reduced to a display which was orderly and comprehensible; the lighting was improved; and a beautiful red pen was provided, with a nib with which one could write a telegram decently without penetrating the paper form. In fact as an eminent publicity expert, Sir William Crawford, put it recently in describing the process, "the giant woke up".

It is the object of these pages first to snapshot the awakened giant in the full exercise of his fresh vitality, and then to take him limb by limb, as it were, showing how each limb performs its individual functions and how these functions have developed from the spasmodic jerks of infancy to the muscular ease and facility of mature gianthood.

There is a post office at John o'Groat's. There is a post office within a stone's throw of Land's End. And between them, from the heart of the country to every distant toe and finger of it, to and fro, outwards and inwards, to and from the ends of the earth, there flows a constant stream of human intercourse, electrical and mechanical, fluctuating but never ceasing, the systems of communications controlled by His Majesty's Postmaster-General.

There are over 24,500 of these post offices in the United Kingdom of Great Britain and Northern Ireland, ranging in size and importance from the great central office in the big city, with its thousands of workers, down to the little village office kept by the grocer or the baker, which only just manages to justify its existence by a certain fixed standard of usefulness. Through these post offices 8,000 million letters and postal packets of all descriptions are shot about the country and delivered every year by 80,000 postmen, a matter of 24 millions on every weekday.

The Postmaster-General not only runs a vast and intricate postal service; he is responsible for the telegraph service and for a telephone service which has, during the last few years, made phenomenal expansion and is still forging ahead and adapting itself as it grows to the needs of a nation which has suddenly become "telephone minded". In addition the Postmaster-General undertakes to remit money to any part of this country and to almost any part of the world; he is a banker with whom one in every four of the population has an account. He gives indispensable co-operation in the working of the social services of the country: for instance, he sells £98 million worth of health and unemployment insurance stamps during the year, pays 220 millions of old age and widows' and orphans' pensions, and dispenses licences of many kinds—for guns and dogs, for wireless sets and brewing operations. He is the largest employer of labour in the country and, last but not least, he is a tax gatherer, since the first charge on his profits is a payment of £10,750,000 a year to the Exchequer as a contribution towards general taxation.

The Postmaster-General of to-day, in fact, controls a very extensive and complicated business, and probably there is no better way of conveying a general impression of his activities, as distinct from a detailed description, than to select two sharply contrasted examples from the 24,500 post offices scattered about the country and to submit them to a quick study of detail.

Let us first, then, get a glimpse of the Post Office life of a big industrial city—Manchester for instance.

The Manchester Post Office never sleeps. It has, of course, its peak hours of activity and periods of comparative quiet, but at every minute of the day and night, year-in, year-out, things are happening and staff is working.

Taking postal activities first, as is their right by virtue of seniority, the most impressive period in the central letter sorting office is between 5 and 10 o'clock in the evening. Postmen come in continuously with the collections from hundreds of posting boxes. A hundred and thirty of the familiar red vans back up to the unloading platform and dump their contents—the postings of big business houses and the night-mail contributions of busy branch offices. About 50 men at two long tables "face up" the letters as they are poured out of the bags and pass them to the stampers. The letters are fed to the stamping machines which obliterate the stamps at the rate of 600 a minute. Then in soundless rubber-wheeled trollies the thousands of letters, postcards and packets are wheeled to the sorting tables where they are seized and sorted, tied up and bagged, and so sent on the first stage of their journey to a destination which may be a few streets away or may be on the other side of the world.

There are 300 sorters on duty in this big room, each with his allotted task, and the "hum" of activity increases to a steady *crescendo* as the time passes; by 9 o'clock it is at its highest pitch, punctuated by the rattle of carrier baskets and the distant calling-over of departing bags. It is all so orderly—an easy-running bit of organisation which can have attained its effect of unbustled smoothness only by careful study and long experience. And the climax? The clear despatch of the night mails—the 600,000 letters posted between 5 and 10 o'clock—on their way to every part of the country. At 10.10 the vans are off to the station, followed after a quarter of an hour by an "express" containing the stragglers and latest postings; the express van will catch up the others at London Road and the station staff will unload them and transfer the hundreds of bags to the waiting train.

After 10 o'clock there is a lull in the sorting office. Men go off duty but many others come on, for there are other, though less important, despatches throughout the night, as well as many arrivals. Manchester, by the way, is one of the few big offices which exchange direct mails with the overseas part of the Empire and with foreign countries.

Head post office, Manchester;
public counter

About 1,500 bags of mails are despatched every week to the Continent, 1,100 to India, Australia and the Far East and 250 to Canada and the United States. In all, letters and parcels dealt with in Manchester, inwards and outwards, number about 13 millions a week, and the number of complaints of delay or misdelivery averages four per million.

Upstairs, over the main sorting office, 120 postmen are working steadily through the night, preparing the incoming mail for local delivery. A lot of the postmen on these more or less sedentary duties are disabled ex-service men; those whose disabilities are serious are excused bag lifting and stair climbing. A big, enthusiastic inspector of postmen is in charge, and in real Lancashire (surely the most cheerful dialect in the world) he reels off statistics and reminiscences. There are 1,400 postmen altogether in the Manchester Town district, he mentions, and 640 of them will, in a few hours, from 5 o'clock onwards, be turning out from their homes to take part in the first delivery.

Manchester, like London, has a system of district numbers for postal purposes. There are 19 districts and the inclusion of the proper number in the address of a letter, of course, facilitates and speeds up sorting enormously. But the Manchester people, or rather their correspondents, have been slow to adopt the numbers and two-thirds of the correspondence is still addressed without them. In a more bureaucratic community there would probably be a deliberate hold-up of letters to bring people into line, but the Manchester Post Office struggles on and hopes for the best.

The temporary lull in the sorting office passes as the inward mails begin to arrive in a steady stream. At 2 o'clock in the morning there is another "peak" of activity. The main inward night mail arrives—350 bags of it—letters posted in London and many other parts of the country the previous evening. There is a rapid check-ing of these bags to see that the due quota is all present and correct, an examining of the lead seals to ensure that they are intact, then the opening of the bags, the checking of registered letters and the disposal of the bundles of letters to the waiting sorters—all these processes, and the sorting which follows, are organised to the last detail to ensure accuracy and an economy of time, for another heavy mail of about 150 bags is due soon after 3 o'clock.

From now on the buzz of activity rises again. The post-men come on duty to prepare their "walks". Vans leave at intervals for the district offices and, at 7 o'clock, from the head office and all its satellites a stream of postmen goes forth, awheel and on foot, so that even in the most distant suburb the morning letters may be all delivered by 8.45. In order to include as many letters as possible in the first delivery, the last vans to the district offices carry bags from the Crewe-to-Manchester sorting carriage—an ex-tension of the Manchester sorting office on wheels which has enabled a local staff to divide the contents of inward bags into the various postal districts before they reach Manchester. As a result letters that reach London Road station after 6 o'clock may actually be delivered to an addressee three or four miles away shortly after 7 o'clock.

Another big building half a mile away is the parcel post centre. Here there is the same activity in the evening as the red vans come in with the vast parcel postings of a city which specialises in mail-order business. But it is a different kind of activity, a different sort of sound. Mechanised aid has been introduced here—this was in fact the first parcel sorting office to be fitted with a mechanical sorter—and as the vans are unloaded at the platform the contents are spilled on to a swiftly moving band which conveys them up to the first floor. Here they are caught by a string of trucks. Each truck as it fills is wheeled to a circle of sorters who sort the parcels into eleven carefully padded holes in the floor. This is the primary sorting. Each aperture gives access to another moving band which conveys the parcels to the various "roads" where they are sorted into their proper bags ready for despatch.

There is the same fluctuation of activity here during the night as at the letter office; the same influx (but on a smaller scale) of postmen in the early morning, culminating in the despatch of 36 vans in all directions to deliver the parcels at their various destinations.

At still another building, this time right in the heart of the city, is Manchester's G.P.O., comprising, with other features of Post Office work, a public office—the shop window, as it were, of the whole concern—which, if not the finest in the country, certainly ranks in the first two or three. The public counter is nearly 200 feet long and it is staffed throughout the day by a trained staff of 70 men and women, about 30 being generally on duty at a time. Considerable training is given behind the scenes before the new entrant is entrusted with a position at the counter, where expert service is expected.

The activity varies in degree and in kind during the day. First thing in the morning, for instance, which at the public counter means 7 o'clock, there is a concentration at one end where the private boxes are situated. Here the messengers from various business houses come to collect their letters. It used to be a sign of substance and respectability to rent a private box; now in many cases it is the observance of a tradition rather than a measure of convenience. Anyhow there are 600 people or firms in Manchester who prefer to send for their correspondence rather than have it delivered. Some of the messengers are small boys just starting on their business career; there is evidence of the usual disposition of small boys to be boisterous, but the budding disturbance is quelled by a more responsible representative, a commissionaire from one of the larger firms; he looks like an ex-sergeant major. The counter clerks and the messengers are well known to each other from regular daily contact and the utmost friendliness prevails.

As 9 o'clock approaches business in the office becomes more active. The telephone sales representative, in an office of his own on the public side of the counter, has arrived and is explaining to a prospective subscriber what a revolution being on the telephone will make in his life—and, on the other hand, what is expected of him as a telephone user. People on their way to work call to buy stamps, send a greetings telegram for a relative's birthday, or put a few shillings away in the Post Office Savings Bank for their holidays—all normal transactions which are quickly disposed of by the counter officers. But here comes a more interesting looking customer, a coloured man, rather distinguished looking in bright headdress, who wishes to send a telegram to the Belgian Congo. After a reference by the counter officer to the relative rates and rules, money passes and the message is whisked up a pneumatic tube and will almost immediately be on its way to Africa.

Next comes a Malay stoker from one of the ships in the Manchester docks. In broken English he confides to the counter officer that he has been paid off and wants to send some money to his wife in Pahang, a town in the Federated Malay States. Will the good gentleman tell him how to do it? The good gentleman by means of the Imperial Money Order service proves helpful, and the stoker hands over his money, without quite knowing what will be done about it but with the certain knowledge that his wife in Pahang will receive the local equivalent of the money which he has entrusted to the British Post Office.

Many types are to be seen from behind the counter

grille as the daily work in each section proceeds. There is the liverish gentleman who continually taps on the counter with his coin and makes audibly offensive remarks about the inefficiency of the staff. He is just as courteously served as the genial little fellow who is waiting with a telegram to a bookie. With a laugh he informs all and sundry that Dying Duck is a certainty for the 3.30.

Farther down a queue waits at the postal order section, for the football season is in full swing and coupons have to be despatched in order that fortunes may be made. Many of the coupons are filled in with Post Office pen and ink at the writing tables which run down the centre of the public office.

Throughout the whole day there is a continuous stream of callers with parcels for India, Australia, Hong Kong, Canada, and all over the world; with telegrams for Abyssinia, South Africa, the Falklands and Fiji, Russia, Germany, Mauritius—these are just a few taken at random; money orders are bought for China, Peru, Japan, Borneo, Aden and Argentine, a steady flow of business of immense variety.

But as 5 o'clock approaches the number of customers swells and from 5 to 6 o'clock the office becomes highly animated, each officer dealing unceasingly with a stream of transactions, simple and complex. Now come the business houses disgorging their mails, people of all types bringing in heavy loads of parcels, packets and letters; all are quickly absorbed and sent to the sorting office for disposal. After 6 o'clock the pressure subsides a little but there is considerable activity up to 11 o'clock, when the last laggard enjoying a rest at one of the well-equipped tables packs up for the night. At 11 o'clock a separate night counter starts business and remains open all night.

There are some curious customers found sometimes haunting the tables in the public office. One seedy old gentleman who spent a good deal of time there had the temerity to complain that the draught from the swing doors had given him a chill. It transpired that he did all the clerical work of his business there and protested strongly when he was warned off.

Another *habitué* in the old days used to spend hours inditing telegrams to the Prime Minister, the Chancellor of the Exchequer and other prominent people. He never sent them, but he would break off now and then to toast a slice of bread at the office fire. He, too, at length had to be evicted and no doubt harbours resentment against a pampered bureaucracy. There is more than a sprinkling of comedy and pathos in the immense amount of human activity which is concentrated in a day's work in the Manchester Post Office.

Upstairs in the telegraph department the day really begins at 7 o'clock. Before that time traffic has been a sluggish trickle of telegrams from railway officials and belated travellers. At 7 o'clock a stir is manifest in the instrument room. A corps of men in yellow overalls is busy cleaning and "tuning up" machinery ready for the day's work. Some machines are already active. Those connected with the great fishing ports—Grimsby, Fleetwood and Aberdeen—are pouring in a flood of quotations, for Manchester is an important centre of distribution. This fish traffic starts very early and its telegrams have a special importance because of the perishable nature of the goods. Generally the messages are in figure code and so to the layman unintelligible.

Just before 9 o'clock the corridors are filled by a kaleidoscopic mob of cheerful, chatty, laughing girls. They "clock in" and sort themselves out and proceed sedately to their appointed posts, for at this hour the instrument room is getting into full swing. Now commences the real business of the day as commercial offices of all kinds become busy. The "hum" of the room rises;

it is a different hum from that in the sorting office. Every business man knows how, instinctively, he can gauge the conditions in his office by this indescribable hum, and so it is with the telegraph superintendent. The note of it goes on rising above the subdued rattle of the machines until, at about 10.30, the morning traffic peak is reached. Nearly 4,000 telegrams are dealt with in that peak hour every day.

The long instrument room shows orderly rows of tele-printers communicating directly with the larger towns. These machines are in effect long-distance typewriters, though this description would probably horrify the engineers. The keyboard is so nearly standard that any expert typist, with a short additional specialised training, can use the instrument quite effectively. The old skilled telegraphist is dying out; in one case a father, highly skilled in Morse and Wheatstone, works side by side with his daughter on new-fangled teleprinters, doubtless with some scorn in his heart. Telegrams can be typed at speeds up to 60 words a minute, and they appear at the distant station printed upon a narrow paper tape ready for gum-ming to the telegram form. The teleprinters are arranged upon twin tables separated by a deep slot, at the bottom of which runs a moving belt. To these belts all telegrams received upon the machines are consigned, and transverse belts carry them to a circulation section for further treat-ment. There is very little handling and no time wasted in walking about from one circuit to another.

In the centre of the room is the London section. There are 10 machines in the London "alley", each dealing with an average of about 70 telegrams in each direction per hour. Near by are similar sections connecting Man-chester with Liverpool, Leeds, Edinburgh and other places. Over in a corner are other instruments available to be brought into use for "special events", like race meetings.

Leaving the teleprinters, one reaches the circulation

and tracing section. Here all telegrams passing through the office are examined and sent upon their several journeys. A telegram wrongly or scantily addressed is not given up as a bad job. Experienced officers, armed with directories and guides of all sorts, carefully examine all such messages, and few indeed are given up as hopeless. Near this section is a long row of pneumatic tubes connecting the instrument room with the public counter and delivery room, branch offices in the city and newspaper offices. Another section of the room, looking very scientific and austere, is "Test", the nerve centre of the telegraph department. It is manned by a few expert technicians who investigate any fault that may appear and maintain electrical and mechanical efficiency.

Through a swing door is a large room occupied by long tables, equipped with cords and pegs, with vertical panels displaying winking lights. This is the telephone-telegram or "phonogram" room, and here are seated perhaps 80 girl operators, each equipped with a personal headset which, when not in use, is stored in its own bag, zip-fastened and numbered. They deal with telegrams to and from subscribers in offices or at home, from customers in kiosks, and also with messages to and from the smaller telegraph offices. The room is quiet after the bustle of the instrument room. Indeed its quietness, considering all the talking that is going on into the mouthpieces, strikes one as almost uncanny; the noise amounts to little more than a mild buzz. The messages received here are typewritten and passed to the circulation section along moving belts.

By 1 o'clock the heavy traffic has somewhat abated, merchants and business men generally are at lunch and there is a comparatively quiet period, matched by a smaller staff. Later there is a second traffic peak as business offices make a spurt to dispose of the day's work. More evident becomes the increasing flow of news traffic.

Manchester has long been regarded by newspaper proprietors as a suitable publishing centre for distribution in
the North. Most of the national dailies publish here a
northern edition, and there are of course important local
newspapers. Their columns are fed by a flood of press
stories coming from all parts of the country. The scene
between 4 and 7 o'clock in the evening is an animated one ;
here is a race meeting at Doncaster absorbing four or
more of the "special-event" teleprinters, there a conference at Hastings, and there a golf championship at St
Andrews. In the summer, May to September, the newspaper traffic may employ as many as 30 teleprinters at a
time, and much of this traffic has subsequently to be
multiplied to several newspapers by carbon copies.
Manchester's press telegrams amount to about 160,000
words a day.

By 7 o'clock most of the work is over. The staff
diminishes, and at 8 o'clock, when all except the largest
offices in the country close, "Test", by pressing a few
switches, concentrates upon one section those remaining
open. There is occasionally an emergency report of an
accident, or an eye-witness account of some sporting
event. Then an effort is made to "catch the press",
usually with success. But gradually the work falls off, and
the staff, now a skeleton of its earlier self, settles down to
clearing up generally and to the humdrum night traffic.
The day's work is over.

Two subsidiary offices are associated with the main
instrument room. In Pall Mall, in a basement under the
Stock Exchange, is a telegraph office specially commis-
sioned to supply the needs of the stock dealers. Here, by
means of teleprinters identical with those at the head
office, the stockbrokers are in direct contact with their
fellows in London. At the Royal Exchange, not very far
away, is found another large public office tucked away in
a very convenient corner site under the great floor of the

Exchange, which accommodates 10,000 members and has a strange resemblance to an ant-hill. This office deals with all classes of public business, but its telegraph work is despatched to the main instrument room by tube. The total volume of work dealt with at this counter is second only to that of the public counter at the head office.

But before finally leaving Manchester's G.P.O. let us look into some of the smaller rooms. Here are the official quarters of the Postmaster Surveyor, his Assistant Postmaster, his Chief Superintendent of Telegraphs and his clerical staff. Here is the accounts branch which supplies cash, stamps and postal orders to all the counters in the Manchester area, and makes up a daily cash account whose figures would surprise the manager of many an important branch bank. Here also are schools, where new entrants are trained for the whole of Lancashire—except Liverpool, which trains its own.

Coming to telephones, it is only partly possible to give a human picture corresponding to that obtainable in the other services, for two-thirds of Manchester telephone subscribers have "gone automatic" and an automatic exchange is about as inhuman an affair as the interior of Big Ben. One has an impression of just gallery after gallery of mechanism, emitting unexpected clicks and glowing with flickering lights, with an occasional engineer in a white overall going round testing.

In Telephone House, Salford, which is incidentally one of the largest commercial buildings in the district, there is accommodation for three of these automatic exchanges, each with 10,000 lines. But the building also houses the Manchester toll and trunk exchanges which will certainly give us the human picture we are after.

The switchroom which contains these two great exchanges, the telephone nerve centre for south-east Lancashire, is 100 yards long and probably the largest in the world. The eye is caught by long rows of polished switch-boards and moving hands, and the ear by the subdued voices of over 200 telephonists. Here again the quietness of the buzz of conversation is surprising, but the room has been specially treated to reduce echo, while each girl is speaking in controlled tones. It reminds one of

> The moan of doves in immemorial elms,
> And murmuring of innumerable bees.

Watching the signals being answered by the rows of operators, with speed but without haste, every movement and phrase designed to avoid waste of time and energy, one marvels at the regularity with which the signals from callers light up. Subscribers, of course, make a certain number of routine calls, but the majority of calls are made as circumstances demand, and the steadiness of the flow seems unnatural. The busiest time of the day is about 10 o'clock in the morning, but after the lunch-time lull the traffic again becomes busy, dying down during the evening until, in the small hours of the morning, only a handful of operators are required. The switchroom is staffed by women during the day and by men at night. Every day 120,000 calls are handled in the toll exchange alone.

The trunk exchange in the other half of the switchroom captures the spirit of the Magic Carpet. The little round brass sockets, or "jacks", marked "Edinburgh", "London" and "Bristol", are actually the termination of wires which travel for hundreds of miles under the city streets, along the main highways, over open moors and across rivers and mountains to the distant towns where they can be extended either to local subscribers or to places still more distant.

The past, present and future are represented by the accounts, traffic and sales branches of the District

Manager's office. What Manchester says to-day it pays
for to-morrow, so far at least as the telephone is concerned. Automatisation has not been limited to the
switchroom, but has extended to the accounts department. Modern labour-saving machinery is employed to
its economical limit, but, even so, 140 men and women are
employed in preparing monthly and quarterly accounts
for more than 60,000 subscribers. 120 million calls are
made in Manchester each year.

That is just a glimpse of the Post Office activities in a
big city to-day. What another quick look round in fifty
years from now would show us, it is impossible to guess.
For all these services are growing constantly and rapidly,
and with them grows the application of constant fresh
developments of science. And a hundred and fifty years
ago the whole of the work of the Manchester Post Office
was done by a postmistress and her daughter, helped by a
couple of postmen!

Now, by way of contrast to the bustle of a big city post
office, let us glance at the life of one of those outposts of
St Martin's-le-Grand known as country sub-offices—not
the smallest of its kind, where the pulse beats so slowly as
to be almost unnoticeable, but one serving a typical piece
of rural England centred in a small market town with
about 2,000 inhabitants.

Helmsley, in Yorkshire, is just such a place. All
around it is some of the finest moorland and dale scenery
in England. The streams abound with fish, and the shoot-
ing, hunting and deer-stalking are famous. Helmsley is
a picturesque little town, showing few signs of changing
times except that the old ancestral home of the landowners, the Earls of Feversham, quite close to the post
office, has now become a girls' school, the present earl
having a newer residence three miles out. The surround-

A country post office

ing country breathes the history of England through its ruined abbeys and castles.

A postmistress looks after the Helmsley Post Office. She is obviously proud of her charge and is kind enough to give us a vivid impression of her duties and responsibilities.

The day's work starts with the arrival of the royal mail van at 6.45 and simultaneously the six postmen come in from their homes to grapple with the principal job of the day. There are generally nine bags of mails; these are checked and opened by the postmistress, and the contents sorted and arranged in order of delivery by the postmen. The first three men to start out are the rural deliverers; their rounds take them over many miles of rough and hilly moorland; some of the outlying villages and hamlets are served by motor van.

In winter Helmsley gets some very severe snowstorms and great difficulty is experienced in reaching these out-lying places. It is one of the postmistress's abiding regrets that once, when the snow lay six feet deep, it was im-possible to reach the village of Hawnby for three days; but there was consolation in the fact that all other places were visited daily and that, as regards Hawnby, the postal van was the last vehicle out after the storm started and the first to get in when it subsided.

The sorting, the checking and listing of registered letters, the making-up of private bags, redirections and other incidental duties proceed until the last postman leaves the office about 7.30. Then there is opportunity for a well-earned breakfast, punctuated by calls to the tele-phone switchboard, for the postmistress is responsible for the telephone exchange as well. It should be explained, before proceeding further with the day's work, that this is not a one-woman business. The postmistress has a competent assistant, and her husband also takes a large share of the work—the responsibility, however, remains hers alone.

A clean-up of the office to get rid of the night-mail *débris* follows breakfast and then, punctually at 9 o'clock, the counter is opened. Friday is the day of greatest activity. It is not only market day, which attracts people from miles around, but it is also old age pensioners' day! Listening to the postmistress's conversation with these aged regular customers one realises the diplomatic difficulties of the work, and admires the suavity with which agreeable relations are maintained. For each pensioner likes to "pass the time o' day", to dispense a bit of gossip and comment on the weather. No matter how many times it is repeated, the bit of gossip always elicits from the tactful postmistress the same measure of shocked surprise; and her opinion of weather, past, present and future, always corresponds, one observes, with that of the visitor —any other course would seriously impede the traffic and cause indignation from the old lady waiting with her pension book half hidden, ready to switch her business to the purchase of a stamp should her neighbour, Mrs X, happen to come in at the critical moment.

Sometimes old age pension business is not so humorous. "Not long ago, just before Christmas," the postmistress tells us, "a pensioner came into the office and produced his pension book. On examination I found he had ten weeks' pension due. I withdrew the orders and got him to sign them, obviously a laboured task. He then said he wanted postal orders for the full amount due. By this time the office was full of people and I was getting just a bit fed up, but when he wanted a registered envelope and asked me to address it for him and fill in the postal orders, I felt it was about the last straw. When I saw the address to which he wanted me to send the registered letter, however, I quickly forgot my irritation towards the old man for any trouble he had given me. It was to the National Institute for the Blind, and I thought that if he was good enough to send ten weeks' pension to such a grand institution, any effort of mine to help him was small compared with his sacrifice."

After the first rush of pensioners come the various bank clerks for their respective letter bags, followed by a few minutes' concentrated bustle in the little sorting office preparing for the outward mail at 10 o'clock. An eccentric and mysterious visit to the counter at this time is that of an old man who walks seven miles in and seven miles out again every Friday to get a ten shilling note changed! Each week he tells the same story. "It's no use going to our post office for change because they never have any!"

Then the market people begin to arrive in town and some of their transactions take a considerable time. They purchase a gun licence, a wireless licence, insurance stamps, a money order—in some cases all these together, and quite often with conversational accompaniment. Some insist on explaining to the patient postmistress (they are not quite so voluble perhaps to her assistant) just why they wish to make a withdrawal from their savings account and how they will try to put it back later— they are almost apologetic about it. Are they afraid of causing an inconvenient drain on public funds or is it that they regard a withdrawal of their money as a little undignified? Senders of racing telegrams insist on telling of their recent gains—seldom of their losses—with detailed description of the running; all convinced that the postmistress is closely interested, as indeed to our eyes she really appears to be.

A farmer, buying insurance stamps, has a warm word or two to say regarding the legislation that makes these purchases necessary; it transpires that he delivers practically the same diatribe every time he comes in. Others, on the same mission, only tender a sum representing their own contribution but not that of the employee. Firm but tactful treatment is necessary in such cases—above all, unfailing good humour.

At intervals the postmistress is summoned to the telephone; information is required which the caller is convinced that she alone can give. During one such digression she has recalled a story which she recounts with a sympathetic twinkle in her eye. A short time back a telephone kiosk was being built in front of the office. Its growth was carefully watched by an old age pensioner and when it was nearly completed he came in and demanded a personal interview. The old man wanted to apply for the job of kiosk attendant and took a lot of convincing that the thing worked without human agency.

So the counter work goes on until the arrival of the afternoon mail at 4.20. This is only delivered in the town area. Two deliverers sort it and are out on their rounds in a quarter of an hour and from now onwards the preparation for the night-mail despatch goes actively forward. With the counter working up to a peak of activity as the hour of despatch approaches, it becomes necessary to be as nearly as possible in two places at once—issuing more licences, selling money orders, accepting a foreign telegram and some foreign parcels, filling in a motor licence application for an itinerant trader who cannot write (still not an uncommon thing in rural districts), helping an old woman to fill up an application for a pension and giving advice on multifarious matters, many of them entirely unconnected with the business of the Postmaster-General.

A diversion occurs. A telegram has been delivered to a gipsy telling fortunes in the market. There is a re-direction fee due and she comes to the office to make a scene. A policeman has to be sent for, and just as the gipsy is removed screaming the postmistress is called to the telephone. A member of the Royal Family, who is staying at a country house near by, desires a telephone call to Buckingham Palace. A nice study in contrasts!

Meanwhile collections have been coming in from the country districts and the town letter boxes. From 5.30 an intense but orderly activity prevails. The letters have to be faced up, date-stamped and sorted into 14 divisions, checked to see that the sorting is correct, tied into bundles and enclosed in bags. There are parcels, too, to be dealt with. The bags are tied and sealed and despatched to the station to catch the 6.26 train. The Royal Mail is now on its way.

Then the accounts must be balanced and the office closed at seven and from that hour till after eleven telephone calls have to be dealt with. Bed about 11.30 ends the busy day but dreams are liable to be broken even then. As the sub-postmistress says good-night to us, she good-humouredly expresses the hope that some unfortunate individual will not be taken ill, or have his motor car stolen, or meet with some calamity which will necessitate for her a trip downstairs to a cold switchboard.

Behind this quick projection of the Post Office at two representative points on its front, one must visualise armies of engineers, a network of travelling post offices and other railway communications, thousands of motor vans and, in short, a great organisation working with the orderliness and precision which alone can ensure efficiency. But before going into further details it will be as well to look into Post Office history and to examine the foundations on which has been constructed the machine which we see to-day.

CHAPTER 2

FROM JEREMIAH TO JAMES II

It is the prophet Jeremiah to whom must be given credit for first warning us of the coming of a postal service. "One post shall run to meet another," he tells us, "and one messenger to meet another to show the King of Babylon that his city is taken at one end."

Archaeologists have contributed more tangible evidence of the antiquity of postal work by bringing to light numerous baked clay tablets and cylinders carrying their messages written in cuneiform characters while the clay was yet wet. And Herodotus, describing about 450 B.C. the messenger system of the Persian kings in their wars against the Greeks, uses words of eulogy which would make any modern Postmaster-General exceedingly pleased with himself. He says:

Now there is no mortal thing faster than these messengers. This is how the Persians contrived it. They aver that men and horses are stationed at intervals, one man and one horse for each day's journey for whatever time it may take. And neither snow nor rain nor heat nor gloom of night stays these couriers from the swift accomplishment of their appointed routes. He who sets out first passes the message on to the second and the second to the third and so on from the next to the next just like a torch race which the Greeks hold in honour of Poseidon. The Persians call this course of the horses "post riding".

In the Middle Ages letters were in the main written only by four classes of the community—courts and govern-ments, the Church, the merchants, and the lawyers; and each class naturally used the system of conveyance and distribution most convenient to its needs. Thus papal bulls and other communications from the Vatican to all parts of the Christian world were conveyed by special couriers, while all monasteries and religious orders main-tained communication with their subordinate establish-ments by means of itinerant monks. Merchants sent their letters, invoices and bills of lading by the captains of the ships or the carriers conveying their goods, while the court maintained a special body of messengers aug-mented to meet the particular needs of the moment.

In England these royal "nuncii" or "cursores" con-stituted a very important branch of the royal establish-ment, and the payments to them form a large and notable item in the household and wardrobe accounts from the earliest period from which these accounts exist. The messengers were employed both in England and in foreign parts, and on affairs of State as well as in the private and confidential business of the Crown and Royal Family, and the individuals attached to the Court. Indeed the "King's messengers" formed the foundation of what, about the time of Henry VIII, or possibly earlier, became a regular establishment under a court officer termed the Master of the Posts.

Brian Tuke is the first official known to have held this post and he is thought to have been in office in 1510. His salary was 100 marks (£66. 13s. 4d.), paid quarterly "at the four usual days of payment in the year", and his duties were to see that horses were provided in sufficient numbers on the main roads to ensure the swift journey from stage to stage, or post to post, of the messengers and court officials travelling on the King's business.

Brian Tuke's post was no sinecure, judging from a

letter which he addressed to Thomas Cromwell, starting "Right Worshipful Sir" and ending humbly "At my poore house, the 17 August, 1533—Al at your commend-ment—Brian Tuke." From the text it is obvious that Cromwell had complained of serious default in the con-veyance of letters and the provision of special messengers, and made it clear that the King desired a substantial im-provement, with "posts laid in all places as most expe-dient and all townships on pain of life to be in readiness and to make such provision of horses at all times as no tract or loss of time be had in that behalf".

It appears from this letter, in which Tuke put up a good defence, that the method of maintaining the post was to appoint persons at certain townships along a main road who, in return for a fee of 1s. a day, would under-take to keep in readiness one or more horses. These horses would be used in two ways, either by a King's messenger travelling "express" or "in commission" all the way with a letter personally entrusted to his care, or by the post himself carrying forward to the next post letters he had received from the post in the rear. When no special person could be obtained to horse the post, when more horses were required owing to pressure of business, or when letters and couriers had to travel over roads not supplied with regular posts, the duty of providing horses on demand and of forwarding letters fell upon the town authorities, and particularly upon the town constable.

The "poore house" from which Tuke wrote, un-doubtedly somewhere in the City of London and possibly at the Windmill in Old Jewry, constituted the first General Post Office. The City was continually called on to pro-vide post horses, particularly for the royal "express" messengers or couriers, and these horses were kept in readiness both by innkeepers and hackneymen, the horses being available for public hire when not required for the use of the posts. These horses not only served to carry the King's messengers and letters, but were also at the disposal of anyone travelling on State business with court authority.

In Elizabeth's reign, under Tuke's successor, Thomas Randolph, the posts were ordered to provide "two horses constantly ready with suitable furniture and at least two bags of leather well lined with baize or cotton and a horn to blow as oft as company was met or four times in every mile." Randolph also fixed the rate of travel at seven miles an hour in summer and five in winter, rates which were maintained, at all events in theory, until the introduction of mail coaches many years later.

These regulations were intended to apply only to letters on royal or State business. The carriage of private letters was allowed, but only on sufferance, and such letters went as "by-letters", which meant that they were not carried unless the post was travelling in ordinary course with State correspondence.

A different set of conditions, however, governed the conveyance of letters between England and foreign parts. Here Elizabeth was determined to see that every letter passed through official channels, and in her proclamation of 1591 she made it clear that she intended to enforce a strict monopoly in the carriage of such letters, whether on private or State business. Clearly she wanted to stop the circulation of subversive correspondence to and from countries with which she was at loggerheads and to impede the development of treasonable plots.

The accession of James I brought the Scottish road into great prominence, and so great was the increase in traffic that one of the new King's first proclamations called upon all concerned to assist the postmasters by the provision of additional horses, "well furnished with saddles, bridles, girts and stirropes with good guides to look to them".

The Master of the Posts to James I was Earl Stanhope.

He had been granted the office by letters patent in 1590 under Elizabeth in succession to Thomas Randolph, and on the accession of James he had received a new patent bringing his son and heir into the office. The terms of Stanhope's appointment were that he should be Master of the Posts within the kingdom as well as in parts beyond the sea *in the King's dominions*. This reference to "parts beyond the sea" when first employed meant Calais, but as this had been lost to England in the reign of Mary, it really meant very little. Nevertheless Stanhope was probably responsible for the transmission of all royal or State letters mainly through Dover and Calais to the various continental courts and, as in the case of the inland posts, he supplemented his normal earnings by charging for the conveyance of any private letters confided to the care of his service.

Unfortunately, despite oft-repeated injunctions, the merchants of such thriving towns as London, Norwich and Hull were not minded to pay 8*d.* a time for the doubtful privilege of sending their letters by Stanhope's service. They much preferred to make their own arrangements and in this they were assisted by the increasing trade with Northern France and the Low Countries which had been fostered by the refugees who fled to England from the religious persecutions. Indeed, it was one of these Flemish merchants, named De Quester, and his son, who, having established themselves in business in London, seem to have organised about 1619 a direct postal service from London to the Netherlands and the countries beyond. So efficiently was this service run that it became an important rival to that of Stanhope. Eventually James conferred upon De Quester and his son the title of Postmaster of England for Foreign parts *out of the King's Dominions*.

This distinction was important and naturally aroused the opposition of Earl Stanhope and his son who foresaw the profits of their office being materially reduced. Young Stanhope, on the death of his father, took up the cudgels in earnest and pressed his case with remarkable energy, causing De Quester to be forcibly restrained, and issuing notices and placards in London warning all merchants against using any but his own service. Legal proceedings were also initiated, and this despite the re-iteration by the King that De Quester's appointment was in order. The proceedings, which were prolonged, at least proved that it was not yet practicable to enforce a State monopoly for overseas posts. But although Stanhope seems to have won the day in the courts, he found it impossible to enforce his rights. De Quester retained his patent, and the Merchant Adventurers of London were also allowed as an act of grace to continue their own private posts to and from their own mart towns and for their own particular correspondence.

We know that the De Questers retained their patent despite the court decision because the elder De Quester, having lost his son, ceded his patent in his old age to two men named William Frizell and Thomas Witherings in 1632.

Very little information is available concerning Frizell, and his shadow merely flits across the scene, but Witherings claims attention as the first of the four outstanding reformers of the British postal service, the others being Ralph Allen, the organiser of cross-posts, John Palmer, the inaugurator of the mail coach system, and Rowland Hill, the father of uniform penny postage.

Thomas Witherings seems to have secured some insight into the business of letter carrying and postal work when employed in the court capacity of "harbinger" to Queen Henrietta Maria, wife of Charles I. Witherings's duties would be somewhat akin to those of a modern billeting officer, in that he had to proceed in advance of the Court and secure suitable lodgings and entertainment. There is little doubt that in so doing he had to set up many temporary messenger services, and had incidentally to forward the Queen's correspondence to her native country of France. His ability in this work—aided possibly by his court influence and his wife's fortune— secured for him, in company with Frizell, the succession to De Quester as Postmaster for the Foreign Posts.

Witherings soon made his presence felt. By 1633 he had organised the first regular packet service to the Continent and had begun to turn his attention to the reform of the inland posts under Stanhope, propounding a scheme by which the State would utilise the existing system of posts as the basis for a public service, charging for the conveyance of letters a postage which would more than cover the annual charge of £3,400 incurred by the King in maintaining the service.

Such a scheme was obviously attractive to a monarch so financially straitened as Charles I, and in 1635—just over 300 years ago—Witherings was granted by royal proclamation the right to settle "a running Post or twoe to run night and day", not only to Edinburgh, but also to Norwich, Chester and Holyhead, Oxford and Bristol, Exeter and Plymouth, with branch or by-posts to towns lying beyond or off the main route.

Stanhope, as was to be expected, resented this further encroachment on his prerogative, and an arrangement under which both he and Witherings were left to use the same roads and the same postmasters for the separate conveyance of State and public letters was bound to lead to friction and confusion. In addition the postmasters resented the loss of their private perquisites under the former system and the merchants opposed the endeavour to force all letters into the official channels.

Witherings's opposition from Stanhope, however, soon vanished, for the latter was forced by the King to surrender his position as postmaster for the State service, and Witherings then assumed complete control of the public and State services both for inland and overseas mails, thus unifying the whole system under one office, with, however, the King's Secretaries, Coke and Windebank, in supreme control.

An interesting commentary is afforded on the times and on the King's financial straits by the petition of Stanhope on quitting office for £1,266. 13s. 4d., being 19 years' "arrears of pay". Stanhope had, however, no doubt made a steady income from the fees paid by the postmasters for their posts and from the conveyance of private letters.

Witherings had not long put his posts in some kind of order when civil war broke out and divided the country into two camps, for and against the King. Although by origin and early upbringing a court follower, Witherings seems to have shown Parliamentarian sympathies. He was certainly removed from his post by the King on a charge of "divers delinquencies and misdemeanours" and replaced by Philip Burlamachi, one of the principal merchants of the City of London, who had advanced a considerable sum in the royal cause. Witherings, however, refused to take his dismissal without protest and, to protect himself, he assigned his interest in his late offices to the Earl of Warwick. Burlamachi on his side placed himself under the care of Edmund Prideaux, a member of the House of Commons who was interested in the possibilities of the Post Office and who later became Attorney-General to Cromwell. The dispute thus resolved itself into a conflict between Warwick, a Peer, and Prideaux, a Commoner, supported by their respective Houses, with Prideaux's agent Burlamachi actually sitting in office.

Prideaux set himself to retrieve the posts from the confusion into which they had fallen, but his task was difficult. The country was still divided, and both King and

Parliament were endeavouring to maintain the letter service in the area under their control and at the same time to hinder the operations of the rival service. While at Oxford, King Charles endeavoured to operate a service to the west, north and south-east with a weekly cross-channel packet service to the Continent via Weymouth and Cherbourg. Naturally, all "deputies", as the local postmasters were now called, who held posts on these roads and were unfavourable to the royal cause, were displaced and the posthouse transferred from their inn or tavern to that of a local innkeeper better disposed. On the Parliamentary side the converse movement occurred, and as the Parliamentary forces gradually spread over the country so the work and responsibilities of the Parliamentarian Post Office in London increased, particularly when it became burdened with the numerous despatches to the armed forces in the field. It was probably on this account that Prideaux—a Parliament man himself—received his appointment as Master of the Posts in 1644.

Matters for Prideaux scarcely became easier on the cessation of hostilities in 1649. All sorts of persons were advancing rival claims to the office of the Inland or Foreign Posts—or both—and a Committee for the Posts set up by the Council of State found it so impracticable to find a solution that it eventually recommended that the two offices should be combined and given out to farm. This meant that the work of running the postal service should be given under contract to the highest satisfactory bidder. In the meantime Prideaux was endeavouring to carry on, but was required by Parliament to pay a sum of £5,000 to the State and in addition to defray the whole cost of the service. In return, of course, he retained all the postage and other income, but found it necessary to raise the minimum postage on a single letter to 6d.

His real trouble, however, came from the opposition or "pirate" postal services which had been openly set up

on the assumption that the State and Prideaux had no exclusive monopoly for conveying letters. The Common
Council of London, for instance, set up a system of posts
on the main roads from London and in particular to
Scotland, thus duplicating the official weekly service. But
the most serious threat came from a specially formed
company, headed by a Mr Oxenbridge, who called
themselves "undertakers". These undertakers actually
operated a service thrice weekly and charged a minimum
postage fee of 2d. a letter for a conveyance of 80 miles
as compared with 6d. under the official weekly service.
Prideaux reduced his rates and increased his services to
correspond, but being unable to compete he was in 1653
compelled to give up business.

For a time the Council of State, *faute de mieux*, was
forced to use these unofficial posts, but it was ultimately
decided to invite tenders for an official service. Seven
tenders were received and the contract was secured by
Captain John Manley for an annual payment of £10,000.
Manley was given the contract for two years as from
June 30, 1653, and that very night, armed with a special
warrant from the Council of State and supported by
troops, he took forcible possession of the Post Office
and of all letters and money in the hands of the irregular
undertakers. During Manley's farm, on the recommendation of the Committee for the Posts, some of the
first cross-country posts were established, from Dover
to Salisbury via Portsmouth and from Lancaster to
Carlisle.

On the expiry of Manley's contract in 1655, Cromwell
gave the office to Mr Secretary Thurloe and this transfer
was followed in 1657 by a very important development
in Post Office history. This was the creation under an Act
of Parliament of a general office to be called "The Post
Office of England" with an officer in control to be called
"Postmaster-General and Comptroller", in whom was

vested the exclusive right of carrying letters and furnishing post horses.

Charles II's accession to the throne was, not unnaturally, made the occasion for clamorous demands from all supporters of the monarchy for a restoration of their former appointments, or for a grant of new ones in reward for past fidelity. The offices of Postmaster-General and of deputy postmasters in the various towns were not exempt from this clamour. Many of the old Royalist "deputies" were restored to their offices, but the chief office of Postmaster-General was leased to Henry Bishop of Henfield, Sussex, who seems to have had something to do with the Post Office under the Commonwealth, for a term of seven years in return for an annual rental of £21,500. This payment, more than twice that made by Manley, in itself indicates the rapid increase in the postal business during the relatively prosperous *régime* of Cromwell.

As the Post Office Act of 1657 had been passed by the Commonwealth Parliament, it was not recognised as valid by the Parliament which recalled Charles II in 1660, so before Henry Bishop could take office as Postmaster-General it became necessary to pass a fresh Act giving the King powers to create one general letter office and to appoint a Postmaster-General. This was the primary object of the Post Office Act of 1660, which, although following in essential details the Cromwellian Act of three years earlier, had certain very important omissions and equally important additions. It omitted, quite naturally, to repeat, as one of the Cromwellian reasons for a State Post Office, "the discovery and prevention of many dangerous and wicked designs which have been and are daily contrived against the peace and welfare of this Commonwealth". This omission, incidentally, made little effective difference in practice, for when in later years the Rye House plot was discovered and when

Charles's successor, the Catholic James II, sitting pre-
cariously on his throne, suspected Protestant moves to
bring over William of Orange to replace him, the posts
were again held up and the letters opened and searched
under royal instructions.

An interesting episode of censorship at a later date
comes to light in a paper entitled *Genealogical Collections concerning the Scottish House of Edgar with a
Memoir of James Edgar, private secretary to the Chevalier
de St George. Printed for the Grampian Club*, 1873. John
Edgar, a nephew of James, was Postmaster-General to
the Prince during his brief occupation of Edinburgh. One
of his duties was to examine all letters leaving the town.
In a letter from a young lady to a friend in the country
she mentioned that the rebels were in the town 1,000
strong. This being nearly the truth, Edgar asked the
Prince whether the letter might be forwarded. "Add an
'o'," was his reply, "and let it go."

Under the Act of 1660, all officers of the Post Office had
to take oaths of allegiance and supremacy, and another
clause, included in the Bill by the Commons but ex-
punged by the Lords, provided for all letters sent by
Members of the Lower House to be "freely and without
any charge unto them safely carried and conveyed by
every letter post". The rejection of this proviso by the
Upper House was not due to any tender regard for the
Post Office revenues, but purely to the fact that Peers'
letters were not included in the privilege. The proviso for
"franking" M.P.'s letters was not included in the Act as
finally passed, but effect was given to the proposal by a
King's warrant giving Peers, Members of Parliament and
certain Officers of State the coveted privilege during the
session of Parliament.

From the beginning this franking system was badly
abused, as the beneficiaries under the arrangement did
not hesitate to send under their personal "frank" or

signature the letters of their friends as well as their own. It may be permissible here to jump ahead so as to obtain a concise history of the franking privilege which led to so much abuse and controversy. The abuse became so marked as time went on that in 1763 Parliament passed an Act making it necessary for the franker to write the full address on the letter in his own handwriting. Despite this, in 1776 the loss of revenue from franked letters reached the startling figure of £119,000, and in 1784 it became necessary, as part of Palmer's big reforms, for the franker to include the full date of the letter, the day, the month and the year, and to post the letter on that date, the franker concerned not being on that day more than 20 miles distant from the office of posting.

Holders of the franking privilege could delegate their authority during ill health, but without any delegation they could frank letters for any business with which they were connected. This led to M.P.'s and Peers being in great demand as board members in banks and commercial houses and they could practically name their own price for undertaking such service. In one day in October 1794 over 100,000 franked bankers' letters passed through the London office. The privilege was completely withdrawn on the introduction of uniform penny postage in 1840. Then even Queen Victoria relinquished, as a gesture, her undoubted prerogative of franking.

The Act of 1660 contains a reference to "coaches", which indicates that regular services by stage coaches were at this time running on the post roads, but apparently not to such an extent as to threaten by their letter-carrying privilege the revenues of the Post Office. Coaches came into use for hire purposes in London in the reign of James I, being drawn by "hackney" horses. So numerous did the coaches become that they bit sadly into the passenger transport business of the Thames watermen between London and Westminster.

The watermen succeeded in limiting the number of coaches by bringing about a system of licences. About 200 of these licences to ply for hire were issued, and it is believed that the coach operators who were unsuccessful in obtaining them left London for towns just outside the City, such as Barnet, Hounslow and Croydon and worked their services inwards, thus originating the stage coach services which in later days extended much farther afield —to Bath in particular—and seriously menaced, by their speedier but irregular letter carrying, the mail services of the Post Office.

One other interesting feature in the Post Office Act of 1660 is the specific reference to the privileges of using their own carriers to carry and recarry letters, enjoyed, no doubt for many years previously, by the Universities of Oxford and Cambridge, and to similar long-standing privileges held by the Cinque Ports and their members, and "the barges of Windsor and Maidenhead in the county of Berkes and all other places". It is clear that the royal monopoly of letter carrying was far from being fully enforced.

Henry Bishop, the Restoration Postmaster-General, received his appointment on the passing of this Act and immediately began his reforms. The additional posts named in the Act were duly established, and an advertisement inserted by the Post Office in the *Mercurius Publicus*, a news-sheet dated April 25/May 2, 1661, shows that Bishop had introduced a specially important innovation into postal practice, nothing less than the use of stamps for postmarking the letters. The notice runs thus: "And to prevent any neglect of the Letter-Caryers in the speedy delivery of Letters from the said [General Post] Office; Its notifyed that the days of the recept of every letter at the Office is printed upon the Letter and the Letter Caryers ought to deliver them the same day in the summer; and the next morning at farthest in the Winter; and if any fayler be complained of at the Post Office it shall be re-dressed." Thus did postmarks begin in this country.

Bishop also established the first recognised "receiving houses", five in number, between Westminster and Fleet Street, probably to provide a facility for lawyers and commercial men whose place of business was at a distance from the General Post Office, then situated on the eastern side of London at the Swan Inn in Bishopsgate. Before the opening of these official receiving houses unauthorised shopkeepers had made a practice of collecting letters and conveying them to the General Post Office at a charge of 1d. each. They also seem to have arranged for the collection of letters at that office for delivery to their clients at the same rate, thus creating the germ of a local penny post service.

Bishop's energy and initiative were revealed not only in the use of postmarks as date-stamps but also in their use as publicity media, just as modern postmarks beg us to "Post Early in the Day". One of the earliest known postmarks is on a letter date-stamped September 19, 1661. It announced that "the Post for all Kent goes every night from the Round House in Love Lane and comes every morninge", while another postmark of a few years later told the public that the "Essex post goes and coms every day". Clearly the posts were beginning to boom and it was felt desirable to focus public attention on the expanding facilities.

Bishop suddenly surrendered his control of the Post Office in the third year of his seven-year contract and was succeeded by Daniel O'Neile, one of the grooms of the Royal Bedchamber. There seems to be no definite record of Bishop's reason for surrendering his patent, but it was probably his inability to recover his full charges, owing to the unexpected development of the franking system and the extensive use of the illicit posts and messenger services which had grown up independently of the Post

Office. There is also reason to think that Bishop was dis-
trusted as a Cromwellian; indeed O'Neile actually states
that "Col. Bishop was turned out for continuing dis-
affected persons in the management of the Post". The
truth probably was that Bishop was still a good Royalist
but that he could not afford to dispense with Roundheads
on whose expert knowledge he had to rely.

O'Neile paid the King the same annual sum as Bishop,
namely £21,500, but he prevailed upon the King to issue
a proclamation enjoining everybody to avoid the use of
all unlicensed letter carriers, and setting up nine officers
as "searchers". These searchers were empowered to
search all persons and vehicles suspected of the illicit
conveyance of letters.

It was during O'Neile's *régime* that London and the
Post Office passed through two great ordeals, the Plague
of 1665 and the Fire of 1666. The staff of the Inland and
Foreign Letter Office about this time consisted of eight
clerks of the road who controlled the despatches and
assessed postage, three foreign office clerks, two receivers of letters at the window, one general accountant
and one sub-accountant, one letter marker or stamper,
one agent "to ryde the several rodes and find out abuse"
and 28 letter carriers or porters—a total staff of 45. James
Hickes, one of the clerks of the Chester Road, has left it
on record that "dureing the late dreadful sickness when
many of the members of the office desert same and when
between 20 and 30 of the members dyed thereof your
petitioner, considering rather the dispatch of your
Majesty's service than the preservation of himselfe and
family, did hazard them all and continued all that woefull
tyme in the said office to give dispatch and conveyance
to your Majesty's letters and pacquetts and to preserve
your revenue ariseing from the same." Thus it looks as
though the plague carried off no less than two-thirds of
the London office establishment.

Precautions were taken against the spread of the plague through the medium of the letter post by steaming the letters over vinegar, while the letter offices were so drastically fumigated morning and night that the clerks could scarcely see each other. The Fire of London, which commenced in Pudding Lane, quite near to the Kentish Road or Foreign Post Office in Love Lane, on September 1, 1666, soon destroyed that office and reached the chief office in Bishopsgate Street two days later. This it also destroyed, partly if not wholly. At all events the *London Gazette* of the day notified the temporary removal of the Inland Letter Office to the "Black Pillars", a tavern in Bridges Street, Covent Garden. After the fire the Inland and Foreign Offices were housed jointly in another building in Bishopsgate, a house previously occupied by Sir Samuel Bernandeston. Here the General Post Office remained until 1678, when, owing to growth of business, it was moved to premises in Lombard Street, previously the town house of Sir Robert Vyner, the famous banker and goldsmith. It remained here for over 150 years—until 1829—when it was removed to the new building in St Martin's-le-Grand, now pulled down but still remembered by many middle-aged Londoners.

During O'Neile's period of office, in 1663, Charles II caused an Act to be passed settling the profits or revenue of the Post Office on his brother James, Duke of York, and his heirs male. The revenue thus settled on James remained with him on his accession in 1685 and was then valued at £65,000. From this time onward the Post Office revenue formed a part of the hereditary revenues of the Crown until the accession of George III, when it was surrendered to the State.

While at the personal disposal of the monarch the Post Office revenue, in common with other similar hereditary revenues, was burdened with payments more or less in perpetuity granted to various persons and their descendants by previous monarchs. For example, James II granted a pension in 1686 to his late brother's erstwhile favourite Barbara Villiers, Duchess of Cleveland, and her successors. This payment was perforce continued to her descendants, the Dukes of Grafton, until 1856 when it was commuted for a lump sum grant of £91,000. The Duke of Marlborough received from Queen Anne a settlement of £5,000 a year from postal revenues for his services, but only for her own lifetime. Parliament was asked to prolong the grant to Marlborough and his heirs in perpetuity but declined to do so.

On the expiry of O'Neile's lease in 1667 the office of Postmaster-General was conferred on Lord Arlington, a great favourite of Charles II. Arlington is thought to have paid £25,000 for his farm or contract, but being a member of the "Cabal" Cabinet and a very busy man he left the actual management of the Post Office to two deputies. One of these deputies named Colonel Roger Whitley appears to have been a very active fellow, and his records and letters constitute some of the most treasured possessions in the archives of the General Post Office and shed a considerable light on the times.

By 1674 Arlington's "rent" for his farm had risen to the high figure of £43,000, some of which, as he was unable to increase postage rates, he sought to recover by cutting costs. He made all the deputies, or postmasters, pay a fine of a year's salary for the privilege of continuing their office, and cut their pay down from a flat rate of £40 to £36 a year in some cases and to £25 in others. He also reduced the wages of the London letter carriers from 10s. to 6s. a week. By these autocratic measures, accompanied by a steady increase in traffic, Arlington probably more than recovered his outlay, but it is clear from contemporary records that he had a disgruntled and discontented staff and a not too-efficient service.

Arlington's farm of the Post Office, originally granted for ten years from midsummer, 1667, was extended by a further grant of the office for life, but from correspondence left by Roger Whitley there is reason to think that the Duke of York, afterwards James II, for a time, at all events, took the Post Office under his personal control. The reason for this is not quite clear, but probably James wanted to run his own business and cut out the middleman. Another reason for the move may have been the desire of the duke to protect his revenues from the serious encroachment just then threatening from the establishment of a penny post in London, which, in defiance of the Postmaster-General's prerogative, had been set up by William Dockwra, a merchant in the City of London, on April 1, 1680. Dockwra divided London and its suburbs into seven large districts with a central sorting office in each. These districts stretched from Westminster to Blackwall and from Hackney to Lambeth, and in them Dockwra appointed some four or five hundred "receivers" at whose establishments letters could be deposited. Messengers collected the letters from these receiving houses every hour and conveyed them to the central or district offices, whence they were either sent out for delivery, or, if necessary, handed over to the General Post Office for transmission to the provinces or abroad. In the central area Dockwra's letter carriers gave something like ten or twelve deliveries a day and carried parcels up to 1 lb. in weight; his service provided a system of registration and compensation for loss up to a limit of £10 per letter. Dockwra also adopted the date-stamping practice inaugurated by Bishop, and improved on it.

This penny post took about a year to get over its teething troubles and by the end of two years was paying its way. So long as no profit accrued, Dockwra was left in relative peace by the authorities in the hope that his innovation would fail financially and thus die of its own accord. When, however, it unexpectedly commenced to show a profit, the Duke of York intervened and invoked the law. Dockwra was cast in damages and his service closed down, but so great was the public need for a local London post that the General Post Office was forced to reorganise and reopen the service as a State institution on lines almost identical with those laid down by its originator.

Dockwra, thus callously robbed of the benefits of his ingenuity, not unnaturally sought compensation, and although unsuccessful in obtaining it from James II was, it is satisfactory to record, more generously treated by William and Mary. He was granted £500 a year for ten years (1690–1700) from the letter money revenue of the General Post Office, and in 1697 was appointed Comptroller of the Penny Post Service, with an additional payment of £200 as salary.

CHAPTER 3

ONWARD TO
ROWLAND HILL

The abdication of James II in 1688 and the accession of
William III marks the end of one epoch in postal history
and the beginning of another. Hitherto, throughout the
period of the Commonwealth and the later Stuarts the
men who held the Post Office, such as Prideaux, Thurloe,
Arlington and Rochester, were all politicians whose
object, apart from the paramount aim of making money,
was to be in a position to control the circulation of news
for their own and their own party's ends. William, in an
effort to detach the Post Office from politics, placed it in
the hands of two joint Postmasters-General, Sir Robert
Cotton and Sir Thomas Frankland. One was a Whig
and the other a Tory, but both were practical business
men and they remained in office together for about
eighteen years. This system of joint Postmasters-General
continued for a period of over a hundred and thirty years
(1690–1823). In the latter year the Earl of Chichester
started the long line of individual appointments.

The accession of William also had a very important
effect on the overseas packet services of the Post Office.
Up to this time, except for a few small vessels specially
chartered or owned by the Post Office for the conveyance
of cross-channel mails to Calais and Ostend from Dover,
to Holland from Harwich and to Ireland from Milford

Haven or Holyhead, official arrangements for the despatch or receipt of overseas mails did not exist. All merchant ships carried, and were expected to carry, letters to and from places overseas not served officially, and on arrival in an English port the captains had to declare their letters to the customs officer and hand them over to the Post Office for delivery. These letters were called "Ship Letters", to distinguish them from letters carried by packet boats. The captain of each vessel was paid by the Post Office 1d. for each letter handed over, more in the nature of a tip or a gesture of encouragement than as a fee to which he had any claim, and this penny, in addition to the appropriate postage, was collected from the addressee on delivery. Outgoing letters for places not officially served, such as Jamaica, India or North America, were collected in coffee houses frequented by merchants, who placed them in bags specially hung there for the purpose, the bags being subsequently handed over to the ships' captains just before they sailed. Here, again, the ship's captain was paid a small fee, but not by the Post Office, the arrangement being entirely private as between the sender and the captain. In 1686 the number of incoming letters handed over to the General Post Office from ships on arrival in this country was over 60,000, and it is doubtful if this by any means represented the total number so carried, many of the letters being delivered by private means. The amount of this foreign correspondence two hundred and fifty years ago seems quite astonishing, and throws a bright light on the enterprise of our merchants in those remote times.

So far as the official service to Holland from Harwich was concerned the boats employed were quite small—two of 60 tons and one of 40 tons burthen—and each had a crew of only six men. William's wars with Louis XIV and the alliance with Holland increased the importance of the Harwich services materially, but at the expense of the

Dover-Calais service which was virtually closed down. The three Harwich vessels were replaced by four larger armed boats each carrying a crew of 50, but as these vessels had a not-unnatural propensity to fight and to court trouble rather than get on with their prime business of carrying the mails, they were replaced under the King's direction by four small boats unarmed, or very lightly armed, but remarkable for their speed. These boats were built for the Post Office with Admiralty assistance and represent the first of the Post-Office-owned packets. They were not regarded with any great favour by their crews, probably on account of the necessity of having to "run for it" instead of to fight, but during the 20 years or so of the Marlborough wars only two of the packets were captured.

Another important development resulting from the war with France and following the closure of the Dover packet route was the inauguration in 1689 of a packet service to Spain from Falmouth. Two boats of about 80 tons—quite small vessels—were employed, each carrying a crew of about 90 men and an armament of 20 guns. This service was a few years later extended to Lisbon and the number of vessels increased. A further official packet service was opened in 1702 to Jamaica and the West Indies. The post office in Jamaica—the first colonial post office to be established—had been inaugurated in 1688, but letters had been taken in both directions by merchant vessels under the "Ship Letter" arrangement.

Following the success of the Harwich packets, Edmund Dummer, the Surveyor to the Royal Navy who had designed them, built some further sloops in order to provide an official service to the West Indies. The early results were so satisfactory that Dummer undertook to perform the service as a contractor to the Post Office for an annual sum of £12,500. His offer was accepted and five boats of about 140 tons burthen and carrying 26 men and 10 guns were provided. Freight and passengers were carried, but in order to cover the cost of the service the postage rates were materially increased. Unfortunately this increase merely reduced the traffic, leaving the receipts from postage not very much greater than under the old rates, and at the end of the first year Dummer, who had lost three of his ships owing either to storm or enemy action, was heavily out of pocket. Probably because he had been instrumental in getting the postage rates increased, the West Indian merchants boycotted his ships for the conveyance of their goods, thus adding to his troubles, and after a vain effort to carry out his contract, Dummer threw in his hand in 1711. He died soon afterwards, bankrupt and heartbroken—a pioneer in the mail services of the British Empire to whom honour is due, however belated.

The outstanding romance of the Post Office packets of the eighteenth century concerns the risks they ran and the fights they fought in their journeys to and from their destinations abroad. Most of the century was a period of war and privateers were always active in their search for the packets with their cargo of mails or, it might be, bullion. Although the packets were lightly armed their safety lay in flight. In fact the instructions to the captains were to fight if fight they must, but to avoid fighting whenever possible, and in no case to go in quest of adventure. In the case of the sea-going Falmouth packets there is considerable evidence that these instructions were more honoured in the breach than in the observance, for records show that the packets not only stood up to their attackers and sometimes came off victors against more heavily armed and manned aggressors, but frequently went out of their way to chase and capture prizes.

Marlborough's campaigns against France had several interesting effects on the British Post Office. For the first time—at all events since the days of Henry V—a large organised army of British troops took the field on the Continent, and not only did it become necessary to increase materially the packet services to the Netherlands, but also to establish lines of posts or mounted couriers to the headquarters of the various armies in the field. This was done in 1709 and many of Marlborough's letters written during the campaign and still preserved at Blenheim must have travelled home to his dear Sarah by this system of field posts. Probably few of those who, in the last War, had cause to appreciate the efficient Army Post Office of the British Expeditionary Force, reflected that the dust-covered lorries, loaded to the top with mail bags, which distributed the soldiers' letters and parcels along the lines of communication, were probably traversing some of the routes set up by Marlborough.

Marlborough's campaigns had incidentally a most serious effect on the revenue of the Post Office. Wars are notoriously expensive and when it becomes necessary to pay for them one of the first services to be tapped for revenue is the Post Office. And so it was in 1710 when Parliament decided that an increase in postage rates was called for. As matters then stood all revenues went to the Crown, but the Post Office Act of 1711, by which the postage rates from London for single letters—that is letters of one sheet—were increased from

> 2d. to 3d. for a conveyance of 80 miles or under,
> 3d. to 4d. for a conveyance above 80 miles,
> 5d. to 6d. to Edinburgh,

also stipulated that the £36,400, which the new rates were expected to produce, should be paid, not to the Crown, but to the Exchequer for the purpose of "carrying on and finishing the present war".

At the end of ten years from the Act of 1711, with its increase in postage rates, although the gross income of the Post Office had gone up from £111,000 to £169,000, increased working expenses had more than off-set this extra profit of £58,000, leaving a net loss of some £3,500.

On the whole, the story of the Post Office from 1711 to the introduction of uniform penny postage is not a happy or inspiring one. The increase in postage rates under the new Act was in reality the commencement of a series of increases—all caused by the urge to raise revenue and to convert postage into taxation. This movement culminated in the dear postage rates imposed to meet the cost of the Napoleonic wars, rates which, with their accompanying and consequential abuses, roused the righteous ire of Rowland Hill and his contemporary advocates of postal reform. Two very important developments of the postal service which occurred during the Georgian period must, however, be dealt with in some detail. They were the expansion of the cross-post system by Ralph Allen (1720–1764) and the foundation of the mail coach service by John Palmer (1782–1793). The former development concerned rather the system of circulation and accounting, and the latter more especially the method of conveying letters. And the persons responsible for both these reforms came from Bath.

Why Bath? The answer is that Bath, during the century in question, was by far the most popular resort for nobility and fashion outside London. Its patrons were precisely those with the ability and leisure to write letters and the money to pay the postage—assuming always that they were unable to avoid paying postage altogether by the use or misuse of the franking system. Furthermore, rooms had to be booked hurriedly and reservations confirmed by the boarding-house keepers and no doubt those who, like Palmer, himself a theatre proprietor, catered for the amusement and entertainment of the visiting nobility had a heavy mail. In short, from a postal viewpoint Bath was one of the most important provincial centres and the Bath road a most important road, carrying not only the Bath traffic but also the traffic to and from the rising western port of Bristol. The postmaster of Bath, with his salary of £150, was the highest paid in the country and the number of letter carriers—three—exceeded that of any other office. The postmaster of Bristol had one letter carrier and was paid £140 a year.

Ralph Allen was brought up in the postal service, his father being an innkeeper at St Blaise, Cornwall, and his grandmother the postmistress of St Columb in the same county. Allen's work as a youth in the post office at the latter place attracted official attention and he was appointed to a minor post in the Bath office. There he made the acquaintance of and married the daughter of General Wade and, when the postmaster died, succeeded to his important office. Allen was even then scarcely 26 years of age, but his knowledge of postal organisation and the various dodges and wiles of the deputy postmasters was probably unrivalled. Despite his youth, Allen offered in 1719 to farm or contract for the by-letters and cross-post letters. By-letters were those which were posted and delivered on the same road short of London, for instance, between Reading and Marlborough: cross-letters were those carried across country from one post road to another, say between Gloucester and Bristol. In neither case were the letters transmitted through London and the by and cross-post revenue was very largely misappropriated by the postmasters rendering false returns and so indirectly augmenting their slender and irregularly paid salaries.

Allen's offer for his first contract was £6,000 a year for a period of seven years, and this was readily accepted by headquarters, representing as it did an excess of £2,000 over the sums the Postmasters-General were getting each year from the local postmasters direct as revenue from the by-letters and cross-post letters. Allen, of course, set himself to recover this £2,000 and more than recover it by tightening the checks on the local postmasters against their understatements of traffic and misappropriations of postage; and in this he was increasingly successful, although not entirely so. Allen's contract was renewed every seven years at an increasing charge until his death in 1764 and in that long spell of 44 years he achieved a virtual revolution in the postal system.

Allen has been described as the only official to make a fortune out of the Post Office. Be this as it may, his fortune at his death was certainly phenomenal, a six-figure one, and he undoubtedly founded it on his postal contracts. But he also had a big share in the development of the Bath stone industry and in the building of Bath, and in his latter years he was one of its richest and most influential citizens.

One of the difficulties of the eighteenth-century postal service which sincerely worried Allen and the officials in London was the frequent robberies of the mails by footpads and highwaymen. The romantic pictures of masked men picturesquely clad and heavily armed holding up the royal mail coach with a polite request to "Stand and deliver" are largely drawn from imagination. Mail coaches were very seldom robbed or interfered with, but the foot and mounted post boys, who were the only conveyors of mails in Allen's time, were consistently the victims of robbers, despite the penalty of death on the gallows which was exacted from every felon captured and convicted. So pressing did the problem become that the Post Office at one stage actually constructed an experimental bullet-proof cart for the conveyance of letters, but even this was stopped and rifled. The truth is that the wholesale disbandment of the large armies, which had served under William III and Marlborough and in the succeeding wars, had filled the countryside with desperate and starving ex-soldiers to whom the post boy and his letters were quite an attractive and easy prey. Actually there is more than a suspicion that the post boys were in some cases in league with the robbers, and it was this state of affairs which gave impetus to the birth of the mail coach in 1784.

John Palmer, the sponsor of the mail coach system, was also a noted citizen of Bath. A distinguished fore-bear, "John Palmere", had represented the town in the Parliament of 1384. In 1742 Palmer's father was a pros-perous brewer and spermaceti merchant living at No. 1 Galloways Buildings—now North Parade Buildings—Bath, and owned two prosperous theatres, one at Bath and another at Bristol. After being educated at Marl-borough Grammar School young Palmer entered his father's business, first as a brewer and then as a manager of the Bath and Bristol theatres—the only two outside London.

It was probably his travels in search of talent and the need for speedy and frequent correspondence in the theatrical and entertainment business that bred in Palmer's mind the idea of postal reform. On every road the mounted post boys were being passed by numerous fast coaches and post chaises, and the public were using these vehicles more and more, not so much to avoid the high postage rates, but rather to obtain the benefits of the greater celerity of transport and delivery. Palmer argued that the mails should be carried by the quickest means, which was the stage coach, and if the guard were armed this could also be made the safest method of transport. But there was one serious drawback to his scheme. All roads used by the mails were "piked", that is they were under the control of some turnpike trust or other who erected under Parliamentary powers toll gates or barriers every few miles. The tolls paid for a carriage-

and-four between Bath and London amounted to 18*s*. or 2*d*. a mile. The post boys, by virtue of their ancient position as carriers of the royal despatches, travelled toll free; the stage coaches which Palmer wanted to use did not. Palmer's idea was to secure exemption from tolls for all coaches carrying mail whether or not they carried passengers and parcels, and to devote the standard rate of 3*d*. a mile hitherto paid to the postmasters for the horsing of the posts to the provision and horsing of the coaches. The privilege of combining the carriage of mails with a toll-free passenger service was, he argued, certain to ensure success.

Palmer advanced his scheme in 1782 and met opposition immediately, not only from the Post Office officials in Lombard Street, but also from unofficial quarters. At the same time he received considerable public support and lost no time in securing political help through an influential friend—John Pratt, afterwards Lord Campden—who had the ear of Pitt, then Chancellor of the Exchequer. Pitt was heartily in favour of the scheme and at the first suitable opportunity he brushed aside all objection and forced the reform on the Post Office. The first mail coach was therefore put on the road from Bristol to London on August 2, 1784 and covered the distance in about 17 hours—for those days a remarkable speed. Owing to Post Office obstruction some months elapsed before another service was started, but in March 1785 the Norwich road was converted, and other services followed in rapid succession. In October 1786 the famous mail coach to York and Edinburgh took the Great North Road.

Palmer, like many another reformer, although urging his reform in the name of the public weal, had his eye on the main chance and openly admitted an ambition to beat Ralph Allen and to make as much as he could financially out of his appointment. He threw up his

4-2

theatrical interests in order the better to devote himself to his new task and set out to force the pace at which his changes should be effected. Here he struck trouble, for, keen and energetic as he was, he was quite untrained in the deliberate but organised methods of a Government department. These were in any event little to his taste and as a consequence Palmer was soon at loggerheads with the Postmasters-General and the permanent officials. He made a stupid blunder by stopping the mail coaches to the south-west of England in a fit of pique, and a violent quarrel ensued. His dismissal followed in 1793. Some years later Palmer received somewhat belatedly a Parliamentary grant of £50,000 and a pension for life for his past services in improving the postal arrangements.

The first mail coaches were merely ordinary coaches or diligences pressed into service, but these proved so unsatisfactory and breakdowns were so frequent that the Post Office very early undertook to provide the coaches itself. These vehicles were of a special type and were manufactured at the coachworks of Mr Vidler, at Millbank, Westminster.

In London, the departure of the mail coaches from the General Post Office in Lombard Street each night (except Sundays) between 8 and 8.20 was a sight of the town. Later, when in 1829 the Post Office was removed to the new building in St Martin's-le-Grand, the sight was even more imposing. Earlier in the evening the coaches, drawn by two horses, were taken from the Millbank yard, where they had been cleaned and greased, to the various City inns such as "The Swan with Two Necks", "The Saracen's Head", "La Belle Sauvage" or "The Bull and Mouth", all near the General Post Office. Here they were horsed with their working team of four splendidly groomed animals and loaded with luggage and passengers. The coaches then took up their station in single file in order of seniority outside the General Post Office. The posting boxes had been closed an hour or so previously and inside the building by the light of numerous oil lamps and tallow candles sorters were fighting against time, sorting, charging and postmarking the letters and news-papers and making up the leather mail bags with their brass labels ready for despatch.

Punctually at 8 p.m. the coaches were called upon in rotation by destination, the mail bags were stowed into the rear boot and, if that were full, under a tarpaulin on the roof. The slamming of the lid of the boot was the signal for departure and with a flick of the long-lashed whip and a jerk of the ribbons the coach rattled away over the cobbles on its journey, as far distant, it might be, as Glasgow or Edinburgh. This wholesale departure of 27 mail coaches each evening naturally attracted crowds of sightseers, newsvendors, hawkers, porters and general hangers-on, while the arrival of the up-coaches in the early morning was heralded by a similar crowd assisted by numbers of hackney coaches. So great did the con-gestion and nuisance become that regulations were passed, and are still in existence, forbidding hackney carriages from standing or plying for hire in the vicinity of the G.P.O. and hawkers and others from loitering on the flagway or pavement.

The mail coach era, although full of incident, was a comparatively short one of just about 50 years, but in that time the traffic had so developed that towards the close the Post Office was at its wits' end to provide accom-modation on the coaches for the loads of mail bags that had to be carried. Travelling had, of course, increased generally. Coaches had multiplied on all roads following the close of the Napoleonic wars and the return of trade and prosperity. Presumably the solution would have been found in duplicating the mail services had the pro-blem not been solved by the invention of the locomotive and the opening of the railways.

The first mail ever carried by railway was that sent from Liverpool to Manchester on November 11, 1830, but it was some years, in fact after the introduction of penny postage, before the use of railways for mail conveyance became at all general. On the road to the north-west the mail coach was, for some time, actually horsed, as of old, to Birmingham and then placed bodily on a flat truck for onward conveyance by rail northwards. Later railway coaches were constructed for mails on lines identical with the road coaches they displaced, even to colour and the position of the guard's seat. But on the railway the guard's position must have been uncomfortably smoky and exposed, and quite unsuited to his royal dignity, so he was soon accommodated inside.

From 1837 onwards the disappearance of the mail coaches became rapid and the last of the London coaches arrived from Norwich and Newmarket on January 6, 1846.

It was in January 1837 that Rowland Hill placed his plan for uniform penny postage before the Government. At this time postage rates had become not only exorbitant but prohibitive, and they led naturally to wholesale abuses. Carriers and stage coach proprietors conveyed letters by the sackload; tradesmen made them up in parcels and sent them on to friends in distant towns who secured their distribution through the local penny post. All sorts of subterfuges were adopted; the post was used only when no other medium could be found and franks were forged with impunity. Postage was almost always payable on delivery and, to use the words of Rowland Hill, based on the experiences of his own family in their straitened days, the letter carrier's rap on the door "was not always welcome, his demand being certain and sometimes inconvenient; the recompense, in the way of news, doubtful".

The Hills themselves had relatives at Haddington; the

lowest postage to this town from Birmingham, where they lived at one time, was thirteen pence halfpenny. They had others at Shrewsbury, but to correspond with these they availed themselves of a local tradesman who sent and received a weekly parcel.

Coleridge told a story in his *Recollections* which illustrates how the Post Office was defrauded: "One day when I had not a shilling which I could spare, I was passing by a cottage not far from Keswick, where a letter carrier was demanding a shilling for a letter, which the woman of the house appeared unwilling to pay, and at last declined to take. I paid the postage, and when the man was out of sight, she told me that the letter was from her son, who took that means of letting her know that he was well; the letter was *not to be paid for*. It was then opened and found to be blank!"

Rowland (afterwards Sir Rowland) Hill was the third son of Thomas Wright Hill, an impecunious Birmingham school teacher of radical opinions. The whole family seems to have been remarkable for a strong intellect, a sense of inventiveness and a disregard for conventions; but these qualities were specially developed in Rowland, being coupled in his case with a pertinacity and self-reliance which never admitted a sense of defeat.

Until the age of thirty-eight Rowland Hill was the virtual head of a successful and in some respects unorthodox type of boys' school run by the family as a co-operative concern originally at Birmingham and later at Bruce Castle, Tottenham. Tiring of this occupation of schoolmaster and desirous of bettering himself, he sought other outlets for his energy and in 1833 obtained the post of secretary to the South Australian Association. He was thus closely associated for a time with Edward Gibbon Wakefield in the scheme for colonising South Australia, one of the most successful examples of mass emigration in history.

Arduous as his duties were in his new post he found time to study the question of postal reform. A detailed study of this led him to conclude that the chief expense in handling letters arose from the system of "taxing" or assessing postage on individual letters at the multifarious rates then in force. The complicated accounting arrangements and the cost of delivery, associated as it was with the collection of postage in coin, also swelled the bill. What astonished him was the relatively insignificant cost of conveyance even for the longest distances.

These conclusions coupled with a scheme for a uniform rate of postage of 1d. per half ounce to be prepaid by the sender were set forth in his plan, of which the Earl of Lichfield, Postmaster-General, said in the House of Lords, "of all the wild and visionary schemes I have ever heard or read of, it is the most extraordinary!" But public support for the scheme was forthcoming almost immediately. Politicians of all shades of opinion, city corporations, the press, industrialists, mercantile associations and religious societies all hailed the proposals, and Parliament, on the motion of Mr Wallace, M.P., also a zealous protagonist of Post Office reform, referred the plan without a debate to a Select Committee of both Houses.

This committee established beyond doubt the crying need for a drastic revision of postage rates, a need which was now admitted even by the officials of the Post Office, who, to put it mildly, had been very conservative in their attitude towards reform. It was on the extent of the change that opinions differed, even on the committee, and the proposal to recommend a uniform rate of postage regardless of distance, which was of course fundamental in Hill's scheme, was only saved by the casting vote of the chairman. The motion that the uniform rate should be 1d. per half ounce was, however, defeated and the lowest rate which the committee could be prevailed upon to accept was 2*d*. per half ounce. A scheme for postal reform on this basis was therefore placed before Parliament in March 1839. The volume of public feeling in its favour was so great that in the course of six days over 200 petitions were placed before the Speaker, and 150 M.P.'s went bodily as a deputation to Lord Melbourne to press not only for the change but for the maximum reduction to the 1*d*. rate of postage. This must have been a pleasant moment for the author of the scheme.

Impressed by these demonstrations the Government decided to propose the uniform penny rate of postage. This was in June 1839, and so fearful was Rowland Hill of his plan not being accepted in its entirety that he prepared a paper, which was subsequently printed and circulated, entitled *On the Collection of Postage by means of Stamps*. In this he described in considerable detail a plan, which he had already explained to the Select Committee on Postage, for securing the prepayment of postage by requiring the senders to enclose their letters in "little bags called envelopes" to be purchased in advance from the Post Office, or to affix to the outside of an unenclosed letter a "small stamped detached label—say about an inch square—which if prepared with a glutinous wash on the back might be attached without a wafer". At the time Rowland Hill had no idea of utilising Queen Victoria's head as a design for the stamp and indeed he placed all his faith in the "little bags called envelopes", reserving the adhesive stamps for exceptional cases.

A resolution to introduce a uniform postage rate of 1*d*. and to abolish the Parliamentary privilege of franking was placed before Parliament in July 1839, and passed by a majority of 102 votes: a Bill giving effect to the resolution was passed through both Houses without a division and received the royal assent on August 17, 1839.

The way was now clear for the introduction of Rowland Hill's great reform but a great deal of spade work had still to be done, work which, in view of the open hostility of Colonel William Leader Maberley, the Secretary, and the other permanent officers of the Post Office, could scarcely be left to them to perform.

Rowland Hill was therefore offered, and he accepted, a temporary two-year appointment at the Treasury as adviser to Mr Baring, the Chancellor of the Exchequer, for the special purpose of inaugurating the new system. The salary at first offered by the Treasury, £500 a year, was increased to £1,500 on Rowland Hill's protest, mainly to give him a suitable status *vis-à-vis* the Postmaster-General.

After a brief trial confined to London, penny postage was made general throughout the country on January 10, 1840. The number of letters despatched at the General Post Office, London, on the first night of the new system was 112,000 and notwithstanding the crush and congestion of work, the waiting public found time to give three cheers for Rowland Hill and the officers of the department as they left.

An important feature of the new scheme was the payment of postage at the time of posting instead of on delivery and, as yet, this, in the absence of stamps and stamped paper and covers, had to be made in cash. The last step in the reform was, therefore, to provide stamps and stamped stationery for sale to the public. For the stamped envelopes and paper William Mulready, R.A., prepared a design which showed Britannia standing behind a somnolent lion and engaged in despatching winged messengers to all quarters of the world. Much to Rowland Hill's surprise, however, the device never caught the public fancy, and huge stocks of the Mulready envelopes and paper were later destroyed or sold at reduced rates for use as advertising circulars. In this matter Hill proved to be surprisingly out of touch with public feeling.

Mails leaving the General Post Office,
1838 and 1938

With the idea of the "adhesive label", originally intended as an emergency device, he had better fortune. The Treasury had offered in September 1839 a prize of £400 for the most suitable design for the label, but although four awards were given, Rowland Hill rejected all the ideas in favour of his own device which consisted of the head of Queen Victoria against a finely engraved background. Labels and stamped stationery were placed on sale for the first time on May 6, 1840, and this date may be accepted as the birthday of philately and of the famous "Queen Victoria 1d. Black" stamp, the mother of all stamps. Owing to the precautions taken forgery of the stamps was never a serious factor, but the ease with which the red obliterating postmark could be removed from the black stamp proved a troublesome problem for some time. Eventually after numerous trials the colour of the stamp or label was made red and the obliterating mark black.

Rowland Hill had predicted that the introduction of the penny post would have no adverse effect on the net revenue of the Post Office. So it was with considerable anxiety that from his desk in the Treasury he noted that, while traffic increased not quite at the rate expected, the working expenses rose inordinately, so that the net revenue of the Post Office dropped in the first year of penny postage from £1,600,000 to £500,000. This naturally meant a serious fall in the Exchequer revenue and came at a time when Lord Melbourne's Government were experiencing financial difficulties in other directions. Partly in consequence the Government resigned and Rowland Hill found himself at the Treasury in the invidious position of an unpopular radical reformer in the midst of Sir Robert Peel's Tory Government and working with a Tory Postmaster-General and an unfriendly Post Office.

The new Ministry did not, however, scrap the plan for

Post Office reform or even modify it, but it did dispense with Rowland Hill's services at the Treasury on the ground that the term of his engagement had expired.

The storm in Parliament which followed led to the setting up of yet another Select Committee on Postage known as the "1843" Committee, but it was not until the Liberal Government returned to power in 1846 that Rowland Hill could make progress in the matter nearest his heart. He filled in the interval very satisfactorily to his finances by joining the Board of Directors of the Brighton Railway Company. The chairman afterwards told him that he had been in some trepidation lest Hill should propose universal penny fares, to the ruin of the company's finances! But he did invent the system of Sunday excursions and became chairman of the company, a position which he resigned in anticipation of being able to resume his work for postal reform at the pending change of Government.

In due course he was in fact re-appointed, not this time to the Treasury, but as Secretary to the Postmaster-General, jointly with Colonel Maberley. This dual arrangement, as might have been anticipated, was not conducive to the smoothest working but on the whole some very satisfactory results were achieved. The penny post was by now, of course, well established and the reformer could look in other directions. For seven years Hill occupied the joint secretaryship; then in 1854 Colonel Maberley's removal to the Audit Office gave him the undivided enjoyment of the appointment of Permanent Head of the Post Office.

The next ten years, until 1864, when he resigned through ill health, were years of outstanding development in all sections of Post Office activities. Registration, the conveyance of mails by railway, the introduction of letter boxes and the book post, reform of the money order system and rural post services, and the foundation of the Post Office Savings Bank are but a few of the changes which can be associated with the name of Rowland Hill, a name which will always be remembered throughout the country and especially in the Post Office. For, to quote his brother's epitaph: "He has done almost more than any other man to bring near those who are far off, to bind the nations together, and to make the whole world kin."

CHAPTER 4

THE ROYAL MAIL TO-DAY. INLAND SERVICES

Though the Post Office in these days covers a considerable number of distinct activities, its primary business still is to get a letter from the posting box into which it has been dropped by a confiding correspondent—one of 88,000 posting boxes throughout the country—to the letter box in the front door of the addressee, which may be in the next street, at the other end of the country, or possibly at the other end of the world, and to do the job as speedily and as economically as possible.

There are some 15,000 post offices in the country at which mails are made up, and each of these offices may have letters for any of the others. Some 8,000 million articles of one kind and another are posted in the year and the problem the Post Office has had to solve is to devise a scheme, applicable to any office in the country, which reduces to a minimum the number of times any particular packet is handled, thereby keeping staff costs low and speeding up transmission.

For the conveyance of inland mails the Post Office still depends chiefly upon the railway system. The Postmaster-General possesses statutory powers dating back to 1838, very soon after the birth of the railway service, but in practice the mail service is regulated by comprehensive contracts between the Postmaster-General and the several companies and has developed into a closely woven network of mail trains covering the country from end to end.

The parcel post is in point of age very junior to the letter post. An international parcel post was established by a Postal Conference in Paris in 1880. At that time Great Britain had no such service, but it has never been our way to lag far behind the rest of the world, and preparations were at once put in hand with the result that, after prolonged negotiations with the railway companies, a Post Office Parcels Post Act was passed in 1882 and an inland parcel service came into operation in the following year. The number of parcels posted annually is now nearly 200 millions.

The mail contracts provide not only for the carriage of mails on all trains on the various systems, but also for the running of Travelling Post Offices, known in the service as "T.P.O.'s"—railway coaches, fitted up as sorting offices, in which the correspondence is sorted *en route*. Sometimes these sorting carriages, with the complementary van accommodation for the stowage of mail bags, constitute an entire train. They deal with all classes of correspondence except parcels, but their only direct contact with the public is the box affixed to the sorting carriage at every station where the train stops, giving the latest possible posting facilities.

The first Travelling Post Office consisted of a horse-box fitted up as a railway carriage and it commenced running experimentally on January 6, 1838, on the Grand Junction Railway between Birmingham and Liverpool, six months after that railway had been opened. It was so successful and afforded so much acceleration for the mails that it was decided at once that the Travelling Post Office must be made a permanent part of the postal organisation. A few months after the experiment was launched, therefore, the first specially constructed carriage, 16 feet long, was built and put on the rails. It was a pigmy affair compared with the most modern coaches, which are 60 feet in length, but even this early contrivance was fitted with apparatus for receiving and despatching mails while travelling at speed, so that while in the intervening hundred years many improvements in the detail of fittings and mechanism have been devised, the principle remains unaltered.

To-day a T.P.O. is running somewhere in the country at every minute of the day and night throughout the week, except for four hours—from 9.10 a.m. to 1.20 p.m. on Sundays. The whole of the United Kingdom is covered by a network of more than 70 of them. It is possible to travel from Plymouth to Helmsdale, in the north of Scotland, by a chain of T.P.O.'s connecting with one another at Bristol, Birmingham, Crewe and Perth, with a maximum interval of 24 minutes at any one junction. The annual mileage covered by the T.P.O.'s is approximately 3,800,000.

The first purely Post Office trains commenced running between London and Bristol on February 1, 1855. To-day there are four: the Down Special on the London, Midland and Scottish Railway which leaves Euston at 8.30 p.m. and arrives at Aberdeen at 7.52 a.m.; the Up Special which leaves Aberdeen at 3.25 p.m. and reaches Euston at 3.55 a.m.; the Great Western T.P.O. Down, leaving Paddington at 10.10 p.m. and arriving at Penzance at 6.21 a.m.; and the Great Western T.P.O. Up which leaves Penzance at 6.45 p.m. and reaches London practically at the same time as the Up Special on the L.M.S. These four trains are the backbone of the inland mail service and nearly the whole night-mail organisation of the Post Office is based on their running.

The Up Special is the largest of them; in fact it is the

largest T.P.O. in the world. It has 16 coaches, deals with 1,800 bags of mail every night and over some parts of the journey has a crew of 80 sorters at work.

The Down Special is the second largest, and a fine sight it presents every night at Euston with its 12 coaches each with "Royal Mail" proudly emblazoned upon it. There are no passengers about but the platform is a scene of activity. For an hour before the time of departure there is a continuous stream of red G.P.O. motor vans bringing in the mails from the London sorting offices and from all the other railway termini, bags from provincial offices in Essex, Middlesex and the other Home Counties—a great proportion of the epistolary outpouring of the South of England.

The vans are unloaded and the contents divided into groups on the platform so that they may be allotted to their proper coach. "Direct bags", that is, mails which will not be opened in transit, are loaded into stowage vans where they will lie—like the mails travelling by any ordinary train—till they reach the station of their destination or the station where they should change. The rest are delivered over to the sorting carriages, to be opened and their contents dealt with as the T.P.O. rushes through the night.

The sorting starts, however, at 7.15, an hour and a quarter before the train starts, and goes steadily on. As the time of departure approaches the late posters hurry on to the platform to post their letters in the late fee box, the last motor van has rolled away, the loading is finished, the rattle of the platform trucks gives place to the ominous hiss of rising steam power. Then at 8.30 sharp the guard signals and the Down Special moves sedately off on its nightly journey of 540 miles.

Inside the sorting carriages the dominant note is one of ordered activity. Each man has his duty, each duty fits into a pattern, there is one object only—the punctual completion of the work over all stages of the journey. On an average some quarter of a million letters are dealt with in this T.P.O. every night and failure to make a complete despatch at every point is very rare. The staff, from long custom, know the road "like the back of their hand"; they know almost by instinct the points at which the various sections of their work must be completed, and when mails are unusually heavy they take special pride in rising to the occasion. The superintendent, passing from carriage to carriage, can see at a glance, also from long acquaintance with the work, whether each particular section of the sorting is as advanced as it should be at any particular stage of the journey.

The mail centre of the country is the railway station at Crewe. A large number of important mail trains, including the Down Special, are timed to meet there about midnight, so as to give connections with each other. In the space of about three hours twenty T.P.O.'s enter and leave Crewe station.

The apparatus for discharging and receiving mails while the train is going at high speed is a fascinating contrivance and as this is the one branch of the Post Office where, in the nature of things, the privilege of inspection can only be granted sparingly, very few people have an opportunity of seeing it actually at work.

Beside the railway track, always of course on the left-hand side, is the ground apparatus. This consists of a standard, looking rather like a gallows, with a net near by. Shortly before the train is due to pass, the pouches containing the mail bags are suspended on the standard, which is turned so that the arms project towards the railway track. Then the ground net is opened to receive the pouches from the sorting carriage. Meanwhile, in the T.P.O., the apparatus officer has prepared his pouches for despatch. He knows the exact position of his train

Loading air mails
The "Down Special" T.P.O.

even on the darkest night, or in the thickest fog, by the sounds he hears. A hollow rumble means a culvert; a sustained roar a railway cutting or a bridge; and so on.

At the proper time he opens the door and fixes his pouches on the despatching arms which are on a level with the floor of the coach. The train approaches the ground apparatus, he pushes down the lever to open his receiving net, swings out the despatching arms. A bell rings in the carriage to warn the other members of the staff not to come too near.

The ground net snatches the pouches from the despatching arms which swing back to their resting position automatically; the incoming bags come crashing aboard and the net is restored to its resting position. The Down Special picks up or discharges mails (often both operations simultaneously) at 33 points on its journey. Trying to the operator's nerves, one would think, that timing of action to a second as the train dashes on at perhaps 70 miles an hour.

The drama and excitement of the T.P.O. are cleverly presented in the film "Night Mail" produced by the G.P.O. Film Unit, under the direction of Mr John Grierson. Thousands of cinema-goers up and down the country have got their first impression of the inner working of the Post Office through seeing this film—by common consent one of the most vivid presentations of the "documentary" film so far seen. In the course of the running commentary the rhythm of the train is cleverly represented by W. H. Auden:

> This is the night mail crossing the border
> Bringing the cheque and the postal order
> Letters for the rich letters for the poor
> The shop at the corner and the girl next door
> Pulling up Beattock a steady climb
> The gradient's against her but she's on time.

5-2

Past cotton grass and moorland boulder
Shovelling white steam over her shoulder
Snorting noisily as she passes
Silent miles of wind-bent grasses
Birds turn their heads as she approaches
Stare from the bushes at her blank-faced coaches
Sheep dogs cannot turn her course
They slumber on with paws across
In the farm she passes no one wakes
But a jug in the bedroom gently shakes....

Letters of thanks letters from banks
Letters of joy from the girl and boy
Receipted bills and invitations
To inspect new stock or visit relations
And applications for situations
And timid lovers' declarations
And gossip gossip from all the nations
News circumstantial news financial
Letters with holiday snaps to enlarge in
Letters with faces scrawled on the margin
Letters from uncles cousins and aunts
Letters to Scotland from the South of France
Letters of condolence to Highlands and Lowlands
Notes from overseas to the Hebrides
Written on paper of every hue
The pink the violet the white and the blue
The chatty the catty the boring adoring
The cold and official and the heart's outpouring
Clever stupid short and long
The typed and the printed and the spelt all wrong.

The normal delivery centre for mails is the "post town", usually the head office of a district; from this point distribution is made to the small country offices in the surrounding district. Post offices such as Norwich and York with a large rural area may have to despatch mails in the very early morning to as many as 150 subordinate offices, and it can easily be realised what a revolution has been made possible by the use of motor vans of high speed and large capacity instead of the old horse vehicles which they replaced.

Before the war practically all Post Office road transport was horse-drawn and provided under contract. It was not till 1919 that the Postmaster-General became the owner of a small fleet of 48 motor vehicles. Since then the fleet of 48 has swollen to 8,000 for postal services alone.

The postal vehicles are all of the familiar red colour. There is one primary colour to which the Post Office has established a definite and indefeasible claim—the red of the letter box and the mail van. The red mail van is the most ubiquitous of vehicles and "pillar box red" has now established itself even in the fashion columns of the newspapers. Incidentally, when the Irish Free State was formed, one of the earliest gestures by the new administration was to paint all their letter boxes green! And green, by the way, is the colour which distinguishes all Post Office engineering vehicles.

Ubiquitous as the red van may be, it would be still more so in London, and the traffic congestion in the metropolis would be even more acute than it is, if it were not for the relief afforded by the Post Office London Railway. The function of the railway is to provide a continuous and rapid transport service for letter and parcel mails between the East and West Ends of London; and in doing so it relieves the London streets of vans which would run in the aggregate more than 2,400 miles a day.

This railway is the only one of its kind in the world and though it was completed in 1927 its existence is still practically unknown to Londoners. It runs, at an average depth of 80 feet below street level, passing under several of the passenger tubes, from the Eastern District Sorting Office in Whitechapel to Paddington. Here are situated the letter and parcel sorting offices for thirteen of the

West End areas (W. 2 to W. 14) and the railway has direct connection by means of conveyors with the G.W.R. station. The intermediate stations are at Liverpool Street, the terminus of the L.N.E.R.; King Edward Building, the concentration office for foreign letter mails and the delivery office for the City; Mount Pleasant, the concentration office for provincial letter mails and for inland and foreign parcel mails; the Western Central and Western District Offices and the Western Parcel Office, where parcels for the West End are dealt with.

The total length is 6½ miles. The platforms vary in length from 90 feet at the Western Parcel Office to 313 feet at Mount Pleasant. Each station is equipped for the expeditious handling of mails, with lifts, spiral chutes and conveyors. The tunnels are nine feet in diameter and have two lines of track with a gauge of two feet. There are no drivers or guards; the trains are operated by switchmen at each station; during the peak periods 40 trains an hour are run at a speed of 35 miles per hour, providing a three-minute service in each direction. A train of two cars carries 120 bags of letter mail or 48 bags of parcel mail. 30,000 bags of mail are transported daily; the yearly total is over 10 million bags and the annual number of train miles is 1,700,000.

The latest stage in the development of the inland mail services is the use of aircraft. In countries of wide extent such as the United States, Canada and India, where distances of thousands of miles have to be covered, it is possible to contemplate in the future the entire replacement of trains by aircraft for the conveyance of letters. In a small country like the United Kingdom, where the longest distance from point to point is measured only in hundreds of miles, it seems probable that the role of the aeroplane as a mail carrier will be to supplement, rather than to replace, the railways. The vast majority of people are in the habit of posting their letters in the late afternoon or evening (a habit which the administration would much like to see modified!) and prefer to receive their incoming letters first thing in the morning. This requirement on the part of the public can be generally catered for by the T.P.O.'s, but aeroplanes, leaving their main centres two or three hours later than the night trains and arriving at other important centres at the same time or earlier, could enable even more letters, and later postings, to reach their destinations in time for the first delivery next morning. This additional facility could only be provided, however, by the use of night-flying aeroplanes and it will not be possible for these to operate with safety and efficiency until the internal air routes and aerodromes in this country have been further lighted and specially equipped.

The ways and means of this development have been under expert examination for a considerable time, and Sir Henry Maybury's Committee on the Development of Civil Aviation has made recommendations which should eventually make the carriage of mails at night by air a practicable proposition. As a first step, it is in mind to run two main night-mail services, one leaving London before midnight and reaching Belfast in the early hours of the morning, and the other leaving London before midnight and arriving in the early morning at an aerodrome serving both Edinburgh and Glasgow. In both cases there would be corresponding services in the reverse direction. Subsequently, further services of this kind are visualised, and the possibility at a later stage of linking up these air services with the night system of T.P.O.'s is also being studied.

But these developments lie in the future. In the autumn of 1934, Sir Kingsley Wood, then Postmaster-General, announced that he was prepared to consider using, for the carriage of mails within the United Kingdom, any regular air service which offered definite and useful acceleration to an appreciable number of letters, at a reasonable cost. This offer led to an examination of the possibilities in conjunction with the various air companies, and as a result a number of useful day air mail services have been established on routes where a stretch of sea has to be crossed, as between Southampton and Jersey.

It is estimated that nearly two tons of letters are carried every day by air within the United Kingdom. There is no charge beyond the ordinary inland postage rates for letters sent by these inland air services, the practice being to send by air all first-class mail, that is, letters and postcards, whenever there is real acceleration to be gained. In other words, the transmission of internal mails by air is regarded by the Post Office as just another form of transport, like railways, ships, or motor vans.

Sea transport, too, is extensively used in the inland services. There are several steamship services carrying mails between the mainland and Ireland, the Isle of Wight, the Channel Islands and the Isle of Man. The Orkneys and Shetlands, the Hebrides and the other western islands are all served by mail steamers under contract, and innumerable smaller craft are employed in carrying letters to the lesser islands.

Such refinements of the postal system as the registered letter and express services need no description here, but it is interesting to know that more than 60 million letters and parcels are registered every year and that the percentage of losses on this total is about ·001.

It is not generally known that persons as well as inanimate objects can be conveyed by express messenger. You can, in fact, post yourself should you wish. Men and women have been posted like letters. The process is quite simple: a form, a fee, and a Post Office messenger to deliver the goods.

A journalist recently walked into Fleet Street Post Office and said: "Kindly post me to Continental and British Airways, Gatwick, and forward me thence to Stockholm." The request proved a little startling at the outset but the officer in charge rose to the occasion. A suitably stamped and franked label was prepared and the necessary fee collected. The label was tied on the arm of the "postal article" who was then placed in the care of an express messenger and duly conveyed by train to Gatwick. Here, the "express packet" was eventually stored snugly with the mailbags and safely delivered at the Stockholm aerodrome.

Another case is on record of a woman journalist who was stranded in a small country town and caused no little excitement by demanding at the local post office that she should be "expressed" back to town. The service was accomplished without difficulty and the lady duly handed over to the London office of her newspaper.

During the stormy days of agitation for franchise for women, two leading suffragettes posted themselves to 10 Downing Street. In this instance, however, the Post Office was thwarted in achieving delivery as the "packets" were refused by the Prime Minister's butler.

Living animals can also be accepted for express delivery, if confined in suitable receptacles, and special arrangements may be made for the conveyance of dogs. Cats and even pet rabbits have at times been "expressed" by parcel post over long distances. But although living creatures are accepted for express handling, they cannot be conveyed by ordinary parcel post unless they happen to be bees, leeches or silkworms, for whose convenience special facilities are provided.

Speed in transmission being so important it is natural that mechanical aids to the treatment of letters should be constantly under examination. The attempts made in this direction by other postal administrations, in Europe, in the United States and in the Dominions, to solve the same problem are closely watched, and a considerable number of experimental installations are in actual operation. The principal field for these experiments is at the Mount Pleasant Office at Clerkenwell, which is probably the largest sorting office in the world. This is gradually becoming more and more like the engine room of a liner.

The latest example of mechanical ingenuity in the sorting office is the "Transorma" letter-sorting machine, which has made a substantial advance towards the elimination of manual operations in the sorting and handling of mail. This ingenious machine receives letters and discharges them into chutes leading into box receptacles by means of carriers operating on an endless track. Each letter put into the machine has the use of one carrier, and the chute into which the letter is discharged is predetermined by the depression of keys on a keyboard at the time of the insertion of the letter. At the Brighton Sorting Office, where the "Transorma" has been introduced experimentally, its potential output is estimated at 30,000 letters an hour.

Although for many operations the skill of the sorter cannot be replaced by mechanical operation, considerable use is made in sorting offices of mechanical conveyors of various kinds for the rapid transfer of letters, packets and parcels from one point to another.

The London Postal Area is naturally the scene of more concentrated activity than any other part of the country. It covers an area of 234 square miles, from Chingford in the north to South Norwood in the south, from Abbey Wood in the east to Hanwell in the west. This area is divided into 10 postal districts: E.C., W.C., W., Paddington, Battersea, S.W., S.E., E., N., and N.W.; except the first three these are split for sorting office purposes into a number of sub-districts totalling 104; the S.E. district is the largest, with 26 sub-districts. There are in all 119 sorting offices in the London area and nearly 1,250 offices where public business is transacted; in addition there are some 6,000 letter boxes.

About 50 millions of letters are posted each week in London, of which 21 millions are for distribution to the provinces. Letters delivered number about 46 millions a week, of which 10 millions are delivered in the E.C. district which consists mainly of the "square mile" occupied by the City. Parcels figures are small beside these; just under a million are posted weekly in London and about half a million delivered, but the parcel post, since the reduction of postage and the increase in the maximum weight permitted, has shown marked signs of increased vitality.

The aim of the administration all the time is to accelerate the journey of a letter to its destination, and not unreasonably it calls for the co-operation of the public in the fulfilment of this object. One step to this end, introduced during the War when postmen were scarce, was the numbering of the sub-districts. This process materially facilitates and accelerates sorting—when the public can be persuaded to include the number in the address of their correspondence! The process of gaining this co-operation has been slow but sure and to-day over 85 per cent of the correspondence delivered in the London area bears the number as part of the address. The London arrangement has been extended, as we have seen, to Manchester; and it exists in certain other big cities in the provinces.

London is always growing and every symptom of development in the London Postal Area is closely watched so that the Post Office may not be behind in giving each new villa or factory the full facilities at its command; it strives in fact to be in front of actual requirements in the provision of new sub-offices, of more posting boxes and the necessary increase in the staff of postmen.

The Regional Director, whose offices are situated in the King Edward Building, opposite St Martin's-le-Grand, is responsible, not only for the management and circulation of all this vast amount of mail matter, but also for the telegraph facilities and all other forms of business transacted at post offices in his area. All the principal T.P.O.'s throughout Great Britain are under the Director's control as well as the Post Office London tube railway. His staff numbers 38,000, which figure includes 16,500 postmen, 8,000 sorters, 1,400 boy messengers and about 2,500 counter clerks and telegraphists of whom about 1,700 are women.

Staff training is a subject in which the London administration has set a good pace and schools similar to the London one, which was established in 1931, are now in full swing at the larger provincial centres also.

The training given is essentially of a practical nature. Post office counters of modern design, with all the necessary fittings and appliances, are provided in each classroom; specimens of all forms and documents met with in the course of counter duties are supplied for use. In order to demonstrate the connection between counter work and the work of other sections of the Post Office, students make visits of inspection to various branches, such as the sorting offices, telephone exchanges and the Money Order and Savings Bank Departments. Also, to bring to mind the recent advances in air mail services, they are taken on visits to the Croydon airport; a flight, however, is not part of the syllabus, which must be very exasperating for them.

In the school each student in turn acts as a counter clerk, under supervision by the instructor, while another student acts as that variable entity known in official parlance as "a member of the public". Dummy letters, packets and parcels are handed in and the transactions are completed just as they would be in actual working conditions. The smallest details have attention. Money is tendered, change is given and sheets of stamps are available so that students may get accustomed to tearing the stamps off correctly. A large number of cards are prepared bearing questions on all conceivable Post Office services likely to be asked across the counter, and students are taught to answer the questions and to find information, accurately and quickly, from various books of reference.

There is no point where the relations between Post Office and public are so severely tested as at the public office counter, and these training schools have helped to bring about a considerable improvement in those relations. The results have been so encouraging that they have led to new methods of training for sorters and postmen. A central school for these grades was set up in 1935 and the experience gained there is being used for planning the training of the postal force throughout the country. The objective is, not only to train in the actual routine of postal duties, but also to stimulate interest in the general working of the Post Office in all directions and branches.

The Christmas season is, of course, the testing time for the Royal Mail. The habit of exchanging greetings seems to bound ahead with giant strides every year. It is no longer just a pleasant custom among personal friends; business houses now send out seasonable messages to their customers and associates; even the Post Office itself becomes imbued with the Christmas spirit and the staffs of the various departments exchange cards of greeting with their *confrères* at home, in foreign countries and throughout the Empire.

Offerings of a more substantial kind leap up in volume year by year as well, setting each year a batch of new parcel post problems. The process of tackling the problem of Christmas traffic goes on to some extent all the year round, the problem differing naturally according to the day of the week on which Christmas Day falls. About October in each year planning gives place to detailed organisation; the administration begins to engage its supplementary man power and transport all over the country; about 90,000 extra men are engaged through the Labour Exchanges; of these some 16,000 are taken by London alone. So that Christmas in the Post Office makes a not inconsiderable dent in the unemployment figure.

As Christmas approaches still nearer preparations are intensified; hundreds of buildings such as church halls are taken over and fitted with sorting frames, bag racks and other requisites. And the Public Relations Department gets busy with its efforts to induce people to "Post Early".

The need for such inducements may be illustrated by a few more figures, though it is realised that astronomical numbers can convey little to the normal mind except for purposes of comparison. The average daily number of letters passing through the inland post on week-days throughout the year is roughly 26 millions and the number of parcels 570,000. On the two days before Christmas Day it is estimated that some 220 million letters and 6 million parcels are handled.

In spite of the Postmaster-General's broadcast appeals, in spite of dramatic pictures of a deluge of mail bags tumbling into sorting offices, in spite of every effort to persuade the public that it is out of all reason to expect a machine suddenly to multiply its normal output by five and retain its full efficiency, the public trustingly persists in posting two days, or even one day, before

Christmas and feeling slightly hurt if its parcels and letters are not delivered by the 25th. For other purposes they are content to regard the Christmas season as spread over a week. The flowing bowl begins to flow about the 19th, the housekeeper who leaves her shopping till Christmas Eve is in danger of being classed as feckless. But a very large proportion of those "compliments of the season" which are entrusted to the Post Office are held up by their senders till the 23rd or 24th.

The Post Office does its level best to live up to this embarrassing trust which is placed in it by a benevolent and festive-minded public. Dozens of special trains are run solely for the carriage of mails, and many an official prayer goes up that there won't be any fog. A million parcel bags are handled during Christmas week at the London railway termini, goods stations as well as passenger stations being buried in good-will—great barricades of bulging canvas, and sweating men with clanging trucks keeping them on the move, striving all night and all day, straining every nerve to prevent the early arrivals being submerged by the late. That is the main problem—to secure a *flow* of mail matter and prevent a stagnant dump, both here at the railway stations and back at the sorting offices; it is easy enough at ordinary times, but when the normal flow becomes a swollen flood, the danger that part of an early mail will be submerged, and thus delayed, is of course very real.

Somehow it is done, with a greater effort in every succeeding year as the Christmas traffic soars upward, with armies of men putting out every ounce of energy over long hours, and always with the most amazing cheerfulness. Notwithstanding all the extra help and all the special trains and all the columns of auxiliary motor transport, nothing short of the true Christmas spirit which year after year pervades the men—and women—of the Post Office would level all those mountains of mails in time for delivery by Christmas Day.

No account of the inland portion of the Royal Mail could be complete without a tribute to the 80,000 postmen who deal more particularly with the first and last stages of its circulation—its collection and its delivery. Doing his "walk" in all sorts of weather, with extraordinary regularity and unfailing good humour, the postman is everywhere liked and appreciated as a most valuable public servant. Only the dogs, for some inscrutable reason, seem to dislike him, and the number of cases in which the dislike takes such active form as to necessitate protective action on the part of the postmaster is considerable.

The present writer, when a young surveying officer, had occasion to call on a distinguished novelist who had complained to the Postmaster-General that a certain postman had attacked and injured a valuable bitch belonging to his wife. (It is generally like that—the dog, in the owner's opinion, is never the aggressor!) The distinguished novelist was not at home, so the caller left his card and so far as he was concerned that, as it happened, ended the matter. But in the complainant's next novel he found his name attached to a singularly objectionable individual with no redeeming characteristics at all. Which illustrates the power of the pen!

There is of course considerable difference between the duties of a town postman and those of a rural postman. The town man usually has a large amount of correspondence to collect and deliver in a relatively small area. Anthony Trollope says the hardest day's work he ever did in his life was accompanying a Glasgow postman on his walk. But the rural postman covers long distances and his calls may be very few and far between. In addition to delivering letters and parcels he acts as a sort of peri-

Collection: country and town

patetic post office, selling stamps, weighing parcels, accepting registered letters, and he will also obtain postal orders for anyone on his round who is unable to get to the post office. The rural postman is in fact, especially in the more remote areas, a highly useful and popular contributor to the amenities of country life.

Again plunging into personal reminiscence the writer recalls an early morning walk with a rural postman deep into the Cheviots. The man suddenly heaved a sigh and expressed with much feeling a devout hope that the size of ladies' hats would soon decrease! On enquiry it came out that a lady living right at the end of his daily walk—seven miles from the post office—was in the habit of getting hats down on approval from London, and the poor postman had to carry them in large boxes both ways until an apparently somewhat difficult customer was suited. At the moment of writing, owing to the modest dimensions of prevailing fashions, the task would not be so arduous as it was in 1910.

The rural postman has undergone certain vicissitudes with the march of time. Once he used in most cases to ride a horse; then he was dragged off his horse or lifted off his feet and put on to a bicycle; now he frequently finds himself scouring the countryside in a light car or on a motor bicycle. As these words are being written a small press paragraph announces the death of the last mounted postman in South Caernarvon, who during his service had covered no less than 277,550 miles.

That we are on the whole a careless people must be the verdict of anyone who makes a tour of the Returned Letter Section at Mount Pleasant. The function of this department is to return to their owners, whenever possible, postal packets of all kinds which for a variety of reasons cannot be delivered.

A good deal of elimination is done locally, so that the

mass of letters and parcels received at the Returned Letter Section by no means represents the whole of the matter which is undeliverable.

Letters which are clearly unreturnable are at once destroyed, but if the writer has been wise enough to furnish his address, or even a part of his address, every effort is made to return the letter to him.

Packets containing articles of value are transferred to a Property Room where they are returned to the sender if possible or stored to await application. If they are not claimed within four months they are sold by auction. The catalogues of these sales, which take place quarterly, make interesting reading. "Overcoat, 4 pairs of trousers and raincoat" for 11s. seems a good bargain if the articles happen to fit, likewise "pair of lady's high top boots and 9 pairs of shoes" for 16s., while "102 leather purses in undervest" for 14s. and "30 shaving brushes, 10 hair brushes and 32 tooth brushes in box" for 9s. would be a bargain no doubt much coveted by a traveller wanting to trade with natives in the Pacific islands. "2 air beds, 2 ground sheets and surf board" in the same catalogue went for £1. 4s. and "71 pairs of scissors and sundries in zip bag" for a mere guinea. Altogether this particular quarterly sale enriched the Exchequer by £200.

Undeliverable parcels of course create a bigger problem than letters. Those which have merely suffered damage in course of post are given hospital treatment and sent on; if repairs are impossible the senders or addressees are asked to collect and if they do not do so the parcels are destroyed. Such as cannot be sent out again are recorded and kept for four months before being sent to the sale room; unless they are perishable, in which case they are kept in the Cool Room, but only until they begin to be unpleasant. Sometimes the contents are puzzling; thus an enquiry for three aluminium megaphones caused some trouble because the missing articles had been recorded as "aluminium jugs without bottoms"!

It might be a profitable venture if the Post Office offered, for a consideration, to pack our parcels for us, or perhaps lease cardboard containers for their safe transit, because very few of us shine as packers, and large numbers of articles become separated from their wrappings; it is not at all unusual to find heavy articles like steel fittings wrapped in the flimsiest of brown paper, tied very loosely with thin string.

The period following Christmas is the busiest of the year, and articles of all kinds pass to the Returned Letter Section—books, chocolates, jewellery, perfumes, bottles of whisky and wine and other things too numerous to mention. Many perishable commodities have to be sold at once to avoid total loss, or destroyed, and the Cool Room is packed with fish, fowls, partridges, pheasants, snipe, venison, wild duck and joints of all kinds. In the main these articles have become undeliverable through inadequate packing.

Many ingenious attempts to evade customs duties come to a futile end here. Cloth samples have been found to contain cigarettes, a newspaper has a silk stocking enclosed in its folds—its fellow will arrive in a later edition. Frequently there come to hand books with a section of the pages hollowed out, and the space so formed filled with articles which should pay duty.

At Christmas a good many letters are received addressed to "Santa Claus" and although, since the address of the sender is enclosed in these cases without fail, the letters should according to rule be "returned to sender", a wise discretion is exercised by those who still retain memories of their own expectant childhood. There is at least one case known where a particularly pathetic petition from a poor child in a slum district was satisfied by a whip-round among some of the staff.

6-2

CHAPTER 5

OVERSEAS MAILS
AND A
WORD ON PHILATELY

Those who claim that internationalism supplies the panacea for all ills can certainly point with pride to the International Postal Service. Most of us use it, few of us ever give a thought to the complicated machinery which is necessary to ensure its smooth working. Indeed it works so smoothly and so efficiently that it makes no noise at all.

It was not always so. The system which existed in the middle of the last century was carried on in conditions which seem to our orderly minds to-day quite chaotic. There was no such thing as a uniform postage rate; charges varied according to the route and the varying costs of transit, and there were often several postage rates for the same destination; sometimes a letter could be prepaid to its destination, in other cases it could not. The *British Postal Guide* of 1856, the first ancestor of the present *Post Office Guide*, contains a table of foreign and colonial postage rates which occupies 16 pages of close print; to-day the prevalent rates can be printed on a page of a stamp book. The lowest rate in those days was 4*d.* per quarter ounce on letters for France; on letters for Germany, Holland or Switzerland the lowest rate was

8*d.*, which covered in some cases half an ounce, and in other cases only a quarter of an ounce. Going farther afield, for many parts of South America the rate was 2*s.* 3*d.* per half ounce, plus a further charge for delivery collected from the addressee.

Not only was the system confusing for the private sender, it was also extremely difficult for the various administrations; in order to compile accurate accounts between the various countries every mail had to be checked in minute detail, and as the traffic increased with the advance of education and the growing complexities of foreign trade, serious delays occurred and there was an ever-increasing mass of complaint.

It was on the initiative of the United States that the first step was taken to get order out of this international confusion. It took the form of a conference of 14 countries, mainly European, which met in Paris in 1863, but owing to the American Civil War and the Franco-German War nothing much was done until, at the instigation of the head of the Prussian Postal Service, Dr von Stephan, the Rowland Hill of the international service, a further congress was held at Berne in 1874. This time 22 States were represented. They adopted an international convention which von Stephan had drawn up on the basis of his experience in organising the German Postal Confederation, and this convention has remained ever since, with slight modification, the basis of the International Postal Service.

The "Postal Union" thus formed grew rapidly. In eight years it included the greater part of the British Empire, most of the Asiatic countries and the Central and South American States. One of the first acts of each new State formed after the War was to adhere to the Postal Union; the Irish Free State joined the year after its formation, Soviet Russia in 1924, and one of the first public acts of the newly formed State of the Vatican was to join the

Postal Union and to send a delegate to the congress held in London in 1929. The Union now embraces the whole world, with the exception of a few isolated places such as remote islands in the Pacific, and is responsible for the handling of some 45,000 million letters every year.

The first article of the convention severed at one stroke all the tangle of red tape and regulations in which the service of 70 years ago had become almost smothered. For the purpose of mutual exchange of correspondence all parties henceforth formed one single territory; in other words—for postal purposes international frontiers simply disappeared. The practical application of this lies in what is known as the doctrine of freedom of transit; every country of the Union has the right to use for its own mails, subject to payment at certain fixed rates, all means of transport, by land, sea or air, which are used by any other country for its own mail service. This is tantamount to a complete pooling of the transport resources of the whole world.

For example, the trans-Atlantic services maintained under contract with the British Post Office are at the disposal of, and are very largely used by, every country which has mails to send to North America. This principle, applied all the world over, gives a remarkable elasticity to the mail service; if any route is unavailable or inconvenient on a particular date, the mails can be switched over without formality to any other route which may be favourable. The detailed accounting which had formerly presented such formidable difficulties was abolished by the Union. Thus the whole of the intolerably complex system of accounting which formerly prevailed has been replaced by a method of extreme simplicity. Countries of origin pay nothing to countries of destination for the handling and delivery of the letters they despatch, it being assumed that the exchange of correspondence between any two countries is so approximately equal as to render accounting unnecessary. The only payments made are in respect of the conveyance of mails in transit by land or sea, and here the amounts payable are decided on the basis of statistics taken every three years.

The principal reform of the Postal Union, apart from this immense simplification of administration and method, was the establishment of uniform maximum rates and limits of size and weight. Incidentally the convention provides for the free redirection of correspondence within the whole area of the Union, in other words throughout the whole world.

A Union comprising all the countries of the world which meets in conference only once in five years must necessarily have a standing executive. This, in the case of the Postal Union, is found in an International Bureau which is maintained at Berne at the cost of the Union but under the immediate supervision of the Swiss Government. The principal duty of this bureau is to prepare, co-ordinate and distribute the great mass of information of general interest which affects the International Postal Service. It also acts as clearing house in the settlement of international postal accounts, publishes a monthly journal in four languages, distributes specimen postage stamps of every new issue in every country and does the secretarial work for congresses.

The expenses of the bureau are shared among the members, who for this purpose are divided into seven classes which share the expenses in ratio varying from 25 units for a first-class power to one unit for the seventh class. It is one of the least expensive offices in the world; the annual cost to a first-class power is about £300, to a seventh-class power it is about £15.

The International Convention empowers countries to form "restricted unions" and to make arrangements among themselves for reductions of postal rates and other improvements in international relations. Under this power the Imperial Penny Postage was established in 1898 and ten years later the scheme was extended to the United States. Though the penny has now become three-halfpence, the principle that the initial Empire charge, and incidentally the American rate, should be identical with the standard inland charge has been maintained.

A long process of evolution in the oversea mail services through the era of sailing packets and steam packets, and then the era of steamship subsidies, brought us to the era of mail contracts.

At the present time the Post Office has contracts with the P. & O. for mails to India, the Far East and Australia, with the Cunard White Star for the United States, with the Canadian Pacific for Canada and the Elder Dempster Line for West Africa. These contracts provide for inclusive annual payments, representing fair payment for services rendered, after taking into account that the contractor is not only obliged to carry the mails but to carry them at fixed times and regular intervals, while the Postmaster-General retains a measure of control over speed and itinerary.

For overseas destinations other than those mentioned, mails are sent by other lines at agreed rates on a user basis. They are shipped on the fastest vessels available and, generally speaking, the more frequent despatches under this non-contract system more than compensate for the absence of fixed dates of despatch. The Post Office issues a "Daily List" which gives full particulars of the despatch of overseas mails.

The first contract between the P. & O. and the Admiralty (acting for the Post Office) was signed on August 22, 1837, and the centenary of this event, which also marked the official founding of the company, was celebrated by Lord Craigmyle and his directors in a manner worthy of P. & O. tradition. In the *Hundred Years'*

History of the P. & O., which Mr Boyd Cable wrote for the occasion, he shows how Arthur Anderson, one of the founders, apart from his commercial instincts, felt keenly the need for cheapening and expediting the mails between scattered communities and families, having been himself in his early days cut off from his own parents by the high cost of letter post. "It may well be", says the historian, "that his personal experience of slow and costly letters first turned his thoughts to the speeding up and cheapening of the posts and so to the securing of the mail contracts on which were based the early fortunes of the P. & O." There is a curious parallel here to the case of Rowland Hill who, as a young man, suffered similarly, and was, just at the time that the P. & O. contract was signed, beginning his struggle for the inland penny post.

Every great mail route has its own story, but the most famous of the surface communications of our Empire is the Indian Mail. Although all first-class mail for Egypt, Palestine, India, Ceylon, Burma, and Malaya is now despatched by air, leaving London four or five times a week, it is the second-class mail—newspapers, printed papers, commercial papers and samples—which accounts for the great bulk of the traffic. Let us take a bird's-eye view of the preparation and progress of this surface section of the Indian Mail.

The scene opens in the Foreign Section at St Martin's-le-Grand on a Thursday afternoon, Thursday being the advertised day of despatch. If bags of mails were allowed to pile up from one Thursday to another the confusion would be awful. Preliminary despatches are therefore made day by day. But it is a persistent habit of the British public to post at the very last moment, and on Thursdays the traffic reaches its peak.

Bags flow into the sorting office in a seemingly endless procession; they are turned out on to long tables and the contents, after being date-stamped, are taken to sorting frames where they are sorted into bags according to their destination. These bags are made up and carefully labelled—a system of coloured labels is used, each port of discharge being allotted a particular colour. The bags are checked and their destination recorded and they are then taken by motor van to Cannon Street station, where they are packed into a special train, each van carrying bags of a certain colour.

In a compartment at the rear of the train sits the officer of the British Post Office who accompanies the mails until they reach Marseilles. The train leaves every Thursday at 8.46 p.m. and on an average will carry between six and seven thousand bags of mails weighing, as a rule, over 150 tons.

Promptly at 10.20 p.m. the train steams along the quay at Dover, and comes to a standstill beside the small cargo boat of the Southern Railway which is to convey the mail to Calais. Here is the scene at the quayside. In an incredibly short time—almost before the train has halted—vans have been unlocked and the crane is swinging aloft and down into the hold. Under the glare of electric lights the work goes rapidly on. The scene is a pleasant and animated one on a fine summer's night, with the sea calmly lapping against the quayside; but when the embarkation takes place in showers of snow, sheets of rain or great gusts of wind or, worse still, any combination of these elements, the aspect is not so pleasing. Be the weather fine or foul, His Majesty's mails must not be hindered; and not later than midnight the little cargo boat is off, full steam ahead, ploughing and dashing through a bitter winter's night or serenely cutting through placid summer seas, across the Channel.

Very soon the towers and revolving lights of Calais loom up out of the darkness, and we sail into the shelter of the harbour mouth; sometimes this is easier said than done, as most of us know only too well. Before long the boat is securely tied up at the quayside opposite the French postal train. Hardly is this done when a swarm of hardy, thick-set local stevedores clamber aboard to unfasten the hatches and set forward the work of disembarking the mail. The bags are unloaded from the ship and loaded on the postal train, and shortly after 4 o'clock in the morning, with a puff and a heave, the Indian Mail train leaves sleeping Calais and starts on its journey across France.

About 8 o'clock in the morning the mail reaches Paris, then southward it goes, changing engines at Laroche and again at Dijon, to Lyons where, about 4.30 in the afternoon, the incoming Indian Mail dashes past on its way to Calais. Then Valence, down the Rhône Valley into the Midi. The Indian Mail is now approaching the last stages of its overland journey. Avignon, Tarascon, Arles—and so to Marseilles just after 10 p.m., right down to the docks and alongside the P. & O. liner. With a sigh, which may express regret at parting with his charge, but more probably relief, the Indian Mail officer from London greets the representative of the Marseilles Post Office in charge of the embarkation.

The work of loading the mail on to the liner goes on through the remainder of the night and into the small hours of the morning. Normally by 4 o'clock on the Saturday morning the whole mail is shipped and signed for. Immediately this is done the ship glides away from the quay carrying with her on the final stage of its journey the Indian Mail, and, as well, mails for Australia and sometimes New Zealand.

The Foreign and Imperial mail services have of course been revolutionised in recent years by the coming of the air mail. The revolution still goes on. Rapid development in the speed and efficiency of aircraft, in ground organisation and, by no means least, in the appetite of the public for speedy delivery of its letters, brings about improvements in the service with a frequency which is almost embarrassing. One realises that with air mails, more than with any other activity of the Post Office, one can only here take a snapshot as it were of things as they are to-day with the uncomfortable feeling that they may have grown almost out of recognition by the time the picture is developed and printed.

The story of the great development of commercial air lines since the War has been often told—how from the first experimental service between London and Paris a great network of air lines connecting up every important centre in Europe has been built up; how from the first experimental air service operated by the Royal Air Force between Cairo and Baghdad has developed that great system constructed by Imperial Airways Ltd. and their associate companies, Indian Trans-Continental Airways, Qantas Empire Airways, Wilson Airways and Rhodesian and Nyasaland Airways, with one great arm stretching from the United Kingdom to Sydney by way of the Near East, India and Malaya, and the other following the course of the Nile and the track of the Great Lakes between the United Kingdom and Durban. Also it has been told how internal air services have been organised in India, Australia and South Africa as invaluable adjuncts to the Imperial trunk routes; how the South Atlantic and the United States have been spanned; and how plans have been laid for conquering the last trunk routes yet un-served by commercial services—those of the North Atlantic and trans-Canada.

Between the years 1920 and 1935 the Post Office used every endeavour to give to its public for the conveyance of its letters the benefit of the rapid aerial development which was taking place. During this period it was the aim to make the sending of an air mail letter an ever simpler and cheaper operation; from the outset the aeroplane was necessarily regarded as a special medium for the carriage of letters and, consequently, charges additional to the ordinary postage had to be made, and the letters themselves had to be marked for air transmission. The years 1920 to 1935 may be called, from the postal point of view, the period of the "surcharge". The endeavour of the Post Office was to issue to likely users regular and up-to-date information about the services available, the saving in time they offered and the postage required; to make the sending of an air mail letter an easy operation by supplying, free of charge, the necessary blue air mail labels and by setting up special blue air mail boxes, both as a reminder that the air mail was at the service of the public and to afford a means whereby letters intended for this express service could be posted up to the last possible moment.

But considerable progress was made in the direction of simplification and reduction of postage, and during the closing years of the period it became possible to send an air mail letter to any European destination at a uniform charge of 4d. for the first ounce and 3d. for subsequent ounces, or only 1½d. per ounce more than the normal postage rates by the ordinary routes. A letter could be sent to any part of the Near East for 3d. per half ounce and to India, Malaya, East and South Africa for 6d. per half ounce. The progressive cheapening of postage rates had the results expected: whereas in 1920 only a handful of letters was sent by air, in 1927 half a million letters were despatched from the United Kingdom, and in 1935 nearly 11 millions. During this period the weight of the air mail despatched increased from 2 tons to 190 tons, and the annual amount paid out by the Post Office for air carriage grew from a few hundred pounds to about half a million.

The system just described still continues in being, but

early in 1936 a new one had begun to replace it. Hitherto
the aeroplane had been regarded as a luxury vehicle, and
air mail as something which had to be paid for specially
by the poster. But in 1936 an important development
took place. In March of that year letters for destinations
on the European services were sent for the first time without surcharge, that is to say, at the ordinary international
rates of 2½d. for the first ounce and 1½d. for each additional
ounce. First a British day air service, operated by British
Airways Ltd., was started to Scandinavia, and in July a
joint Anglo-Scandinavian night service was added, all
letters and postcards addressed to the Scandinavian
countries being forwarded by these services without any
charge beyond the ordinary postage. These services were
followed by others, including an Anglo-German night
service to Berlin via Cologne and Hanover, and day
services to Switzerland, Paris and Brussels. Now, first-
class mail for the whole of Europe, except Malta,
Gibraltar, Portugal and Spain, prepaid at the ordinary
international rates of postage is despatched on week-days
by air or surface route, whichever affords the quicker
delivery. The aeroplane has, indeed, so far as mails are
concerned, ceased to be an extraordinary type of vehicle,
and is regarded by the Post Office in the same light as an
express train or boat. In 1936, the number of letters
despatched by air had risen to nearly 19 millions.

Even more remarkable developments have taken place
in the sphere of inter-Empire postal communication with
the coming of the Empire Air Mail, which provides for
the exchange by air as the normal means of transmission
of all first-class mail between this country and the
countries which participate in the scheme.

In view of the magnitude of this scheme, it was necessary to arrange for its introduction in three separate
stages. The first stage, on the route to South Africa, was
introduced in June 1937, the second stage, embracing

*Sorters at Mount Pleasant, London
Stamp-cancelling machine*

the route to India, Burma and Malaya, came into operation in February 1938 and the final stage to Australia was inaugurated on July 28, 1938. It is anticipated at the time of writing that an air service to New Zealand and Hong Kong will be in operation within a few months. Eventually there should be three all-air services a week to those places. The postage rates charged in this country are 1½d. per half ounce for letters and 1d. each for postcards.

In place of the former once weekly surface mail to most of the countries concerned there are now three air services a week to East Africa, two to South Africa, five to Palestine, India and Ceylon, and three to Burma, Malaya and Australia.

At the present time the load of first-class mail despatched from this country on the route to South Africa is of the order of five tons weekly and on the route to India and Malaya about eight tons. When the full Empire scheme is in operation it is expected that between 1,100 and 1,200 tons of first-class mail will be carried by the air services from this country.

Though technical difficulties, as well as questions of finance, still have to be solved, the ultimate intention is that the improvements which are now being provided in Europe, Asia, Africa and Australia shall one day be extended to British first-class mail addressed to places in the western hemisphere. It will, however, be necessary, when the Transatlantic air services are working, to require the public, at any rate in the earlier stages, to pay surcharges on their air letters.

There are now Air Parcel services, as well as letter services, to most of the countries in Europe. Apart from the speedy transmission afforded, there is the additional attraction that air parcels usually get exceptionally rapid customs treatment.

These are the facts about the Flying Mails as they are

to-day; but one thing more should be recorded about the Empire Air Mail Scheme. Although there was, naturally, a good deal of team work from the beginning, the plan originated in the brain of Mr S. A. Dismore, the Assistant General Manager of Imperial Airways.

An account of the oversea mails would obviously be incomplete without a word about the postal services designed for troops on active service. It is impossible to assess the comfort it brought to troops during the War, and, from a purely military point of view, the degree to which it benefited their *morale*, to have a speedy and regular postal service between every unit in the various theatres of the War and—Home. Even after the lapse of years there can be scarcely an ex-soldier, or a soldier's family, who cannot recall with gratitude the efficiency of the Army Postal Service and what it meant to them.

The service was not exactly the brilliant improvisation that many people thought. Its history in fact goes back to the Napoleonic wars, and there is on record in the Post Office archives a vivid report by a postal official who was sent in 1799 to supervise the postal arrangements of the British troops then in Holland.

Post Office staff was also engaged with the troops in the Crimea, but the Army Post Office on modern lines was first established in the Egyptian campaign of 1882 and was continued and developed in the South African War. Experience gained in the latter campaign led to the establishment of a definite military unit, the Royal Engineers, Postal Section, Special Reserve, recruited entirely from Post Office personnel. This unit, which is a permanent one, has since 1902 kept in touch with actual field conditions by carrying on the postal service for troops on manœuvres, and at the outbreak of the Great War, with an organisation remodelled as recently as 1913 by Colonel (afterwards Brigadier-General) W. Price, it took the field with 10 officers and 290 other ranks. This small nucleus expanded with the expansion of the army itself; each new formation, each new expedition took out its postal complement; the Dardanelles, Egypt, Salonica, East Africa, Italy and North Russia were in turn provided with a complete army postal service, and at the end of the war the aggregate strength of the service in all theatres was nearly 4,000, of whom 51 officers and 2,980 other ranks were in the B.E.F. Ian Hay, in *The Willing Horse*, puts it on record that "The Postal Service of the British Expeditionary Force was one of the un-advertised marvels of the War."

The outward mails were sorted at the Depot of the Service, which began with a staff of 30 and gradually increased to a total of 2,500 of whom 1,200 were women. As the new armies took the field, the Home Depot out-grew the various Post Office premises in which it was originally housed, and in 1915 a temporary building covering five acres of ground was put up in Regent's Park and this was devoted to the sorting of army parcels alone. Eventually a system of decentralisation was set up by which much of the work was transferred to the larger provincial offices. Separate mails were made up for every unit, however small, in all the oversea armies wherever they were serving, and each bag was given a code label denoting the field post office or other destination to which it was to be forwarded. In principle the dis-tribution, after the arrival of the mail at the Advanced Base Post Office, followed the same system as the supply of rations. The mails, accompanied by a guard, were sent to railheads where they were transferred to the postal lorries of the various supply columns which conveyed them to supply refilling points. There the field post offices attached to the divisional and other trains took them over and handed them to unit post orderlies for delivery to the addressees.

In addition to dealing with mails, both incoming and outgoing, army post offices undertook the ordinary Post Office services; they cashed postal orders and money orders, they registered letters, accepted Savings Bank deposits, and sold War Savings Certificates, and it is on record that at least one dog licence was sold! One of the many illuminating facts that emerge from a study of the records is that from July 1916 to June 1919 the troops in France bought 9 million postal orders to the value of £6,200,000 and received 7,366,000 to the value of £2,400,000.

An enormous volume of mail was handled by the Army Post Office. When the man power in the field was at its maximum some 12 million letters and a million parcels were sent out every week, and the traffic rose at Christmas to a level which taxed all the resources of the service, both in personnel and transport, to handle successfully. In the four weeks preceding Christmas 1916 nearly 4,750,000 parcels were despatched to France alone.

However capable and painstaking the personnel, adequate transport was the key to successful execution and in this respect, to quote Brigadier-General Sir Frederic Williamson, Director of Army Postal Services in London (whose achievements in this post can be compared only with his brilliant direction of the normal postal services in peace time), "unstinted assistance was given by both naval and military authorities. A daily service was provided across the Channel to France; for more distant theatres, ships of every kind which could convey mails carried their full complement; and on land the organisation of both railway and road transport almost reached the level of an efficient postal service in times of peace."

The Dardanelles expedition presented the greatest difficulties; the mails were despatched via Port Said and Alexandria, whence they were conveyed by any available transport to Mudros; from there by minesweepers, lighters or trawlers to the three beaches of Gallipoli, all of which were covered by Turkish gunfire; thence they were distributed to the troops as circumstances permitted.

The loss of army mails by accident or enemy action was singularly rare. The first such occurrence in the British Expeditionary Force was in December 1914, when a postal truck containing 50 bags of mails was burnt in a railway collision; in January 1916, a field post office at Suzanne on the Somme was destroyed by shell fire; two months later 37 bags were lost when the packet steamer "Sussex" was torpedoed. In June the army post office near Poperinghe was heavily shelled and a lorry standing outside, loaded with mails, was struck and set on fire, and in August another railway accident accounted for 26 more bags. In the last two years of the War mails were lost once by a railway accident and on seven occasions by enemy action. This list, taken from the *Official History of the War*, is not a bad record when it is recalled that the number of mail bags sent across the Channel to the army in France or Belgium amounted in the aggregate to nearly 20 millions.

The annals of the Army Postal Service have still to be rendered that justice which is their due, and when this is done many incidents of human interest will come to light. Just two of them may be quoted here.

During the first winter there were several references in the Press to the sad lot of "lonely soldiers" who had no friends to communicate with them. One enterprising driver in the Royal Field Artillery wrote to a London newspaper "telling the tale". The immediate result was extremely embarrassing not only to the writer but to the Army Postal Service, for 3,000 letters and seven bags of parcels promptly arrived for him from sympathetic readers. The officer commanding the battery in which the man was serving, unsympathetic soul, refused to accept delivery of this enormous mass of mail, and, at the request of the addressee, who had by now satisfied any doubt he may have had of public sympathy, the parcels were distributed among patients at the base hospitals.

The other incident, which speaks for itself, records the receipt of a postcard by an officer of the service. It was sent from Homerton in East London and was addressed to "The Superintendents of the Post Office for Soldiers Letters all along the Line to France" asking them to "Axept my kind wishes and Gratitude for all your care of my sons letters and parcels you have forwarded to my only child for three years".

Foreign mails naturally suggest the subject of stamps. It is 100 years since Rowland Hill, by inventing the postage stamp, inaugurated a new art, a new hobby, a new industry, a new passion which has swept over the world and was never so popular as it is to-day. The philatelist is not confined to any particular section of society. Schoolboys and kings may be equally susceptible. King George V started stamp collecting as a boy and grew into a most knowledgeable expert. In the magnificent collection which he left there is a certain 2d. blue Mauritius which he bought years ago for £1,450; it is to-day valued at £5,000. King Alfonso, King Leopold and President Roosevelt are other keen collectors.

The process of production was at first imperfect, so that experts can identify no less than 3,000 varieties of the first stamp of all—the famous "1d. black". The writer was privileged to share the thrill experienced by a friend who, buying an old bureau from a curio dealer, discovered in it a secret drawer full of letters each bearing the 1d. black stamp. Romantic discoveries of philatelic curiosities still figure from time to time in the news. Quite recently three cut stamps were found in the office of a solicitor at Hull. They were 2d. stamps cut in half and made to serve for 1d. An obliging post office had accepted them at that value and duly date-stamped and delivered the letters to which they were affixed. The post-mark on one is March 27, 1841, and another January 11, 1842, very soon after the adhesive stamp had come into use. It is not known how many stamps were cut in this way but the specimens just discovered are valued very highly.

The standard varieties of stamps issued by all countries now number something like 32,000, and new issues are being turned out at the rate of about 1,500 a year, so that the collector finds life more and more complicated. In the midst of increasing varieties and types, however, there will always remain the romantic possibility, however re-mote, of discovering one of the great rarities, like the one-cent British Guiana which is valued at something like £10,000; the only copy anyone knows about at present exists in the strong room of a New York bank. The early Hawaiian stamps are among the greatest rarities. A visitor discovered in a disused building in Honolulu an old newspaper wrapper on which were stuck two of the rare two-cent stamps of this issue, now catalogued at £4,500.

It is probably the rapid growth of air mails which has given such a stimulus to philately in the last few years. But while many other countries have issued stamps to commemorate each new development of the service, the United Kingdom has rather proudly abstained, because, however pleasing (or displeasing) to the philatelist, such special stamp issues, in the opinion of our own authorities, only introduce an unnecessary complication into actual working conditions. In other words the British Post Office only issues a new stamp when there is actual postal need for it. The exceptions to this general rule are oc-casions of the first importance, such as the Coronation.

Philately has, of course, its own literature, its own press, and its own body of experts. There is, certainly, a subtle fascination in a pursuit which may lead to an adventure like the following: A young man walked casually into a North London post office to buy a 2½d. stamp. The King George V Jubilee issue was on sale and he suspected that the stamp sold to him was not of the orthodox shade of blue. He bought up the remainder of the stock, some 300, at face value and sold them for £1,500. Single specimens from this small "freak" issue have since been sold at prices up to 50 guineas!

And finally may perhaps be quoted the testimony of a lady who recently sought a divorce in the Vienna courts. "The marriage", she testified, "was perfectly happy for 15 years. After that I became a stamp-album widow!"

CHAPTER 6

THE ADVANCE OF THE TELEPHONE

The telephone was invented by a Scotsman resident in the United States, so both Scotland and America can claim a share of the honours—or at least the responsibility—for a development which must rank with the internal combustion engine as the most revolutionary influence in our social life.

It was at the age of 23 that Alexander Graham Bell emigrated to Ontario for his health's sake, being threatened with tuberculosis; there, at Brantford, near Toronto, he carried out many of his experiments in the development of the telephone, but it was in 1875, three years later, at Boston, where he had gone to teach elocution and develop methods of teaching the deaf and dumb, that a happy accident made him the inventor of the first practical device for transmitting speech.

Elisha Gray, of Chicago, however, ran him very close and, as a matter of fact, Graham Bell's application for telephone patents was lodged in the American Patent Office only an hour or two before Gray's. The question of priority was subsequently contested in the law courts and ended in a compromise, both patents being ultimately acquired by one company.

This was only one of a long series of legal disputes by which the development of the telephone was marked, especially in Great Britain, for the next 30 years, until at length it became a Government monopoly. It is possible here to pick out only a few of the red-letter days in that long intervening period. In 1877 Graham Bell came to London, and, helped by Sir William Preece, Electrician to the Post Office, exhibited his invention to the British Association and to the London Society of Telegraph Engineers.

A month or two later the inventor was at Osborne House, explaining it to Queen Victoria and helping her to converse with Sir Thomas Biddulph a few hundred yards away at Osborne Cottage. The Queen wanted to purchase the two instruments and wires which had been used, but Graham Bell, like a true courtier, said they were ordinary commercial instruments and offered instead a special set made expressly for the Queen's use. A week later again, on January 22, 1878, a portion of a debate in the House of Commons was telephoned from the Press Gallery to the office of the *Daily News* in Bouverie Street; this seemed at the time to verge on the miraculous.

The Post Office having failed to grasp the opportunity which Graham Bell offered, it was left to "The Telephone Company", the first of several commercial organisations, to exploit the invention, and to open the first exchange in London, in August 1879, at 36 Coleman Street, in the City, with seven or eight subscribers. Manchester ran it close for priority; there is indeed considerable doubt as to which was open first because in those days the new scientific toy was not taken very seriously and there are no authentic records to decide the question.

The establishment of the Edison Telephone Company in August 1879 started a short spell of intensive competition. It was with this company that Mr George Bernard Shaw made what he describes as his last attempt to earn an honest living. The company was formed, he tells us, "to exploit in London an ingenious invention by Thomas Alva Edison—a much too ingenious invention, as it proved, being nothing less than a telephone of such stentorian efficiency that it bellowed your most private communications all over the house instead of whispering them with some sort of discretion." He remained with the company "laying the foundations of Mr Edison's London reputation" until the amalgamation of the Bell and Edison Companies into a "United Telephone Company" in 1880.

It was at this time that the first *Telephone Directory* appeared; it showed seven exchanges, or projected exchanges, in London, and others in the leading provincial cities; there were in all 407 subscribers, 18 of whom contributed testimonials. "Your telephones", testified one firm, "have been in constant use since June last, and we have found them work to our entire satisfaction. We have pleasure in recommending them."

Shortly after the formation of the United Telephone Company the Government, growing alarmed at the danger to the telegraph service threatened by the new invention, succeeded in obtaining judgment for the Crown in the Exchequer Division of the High Court that a telephone was a "telegraph" within the meaning of the Telegraph Acts, and that telephonic conversations were infringements of the exclusive privilege of transmitting telegrams granted to the Postmaster-General by the Act of 1869. At the same time the Attorney-General assured the court that the Postmaster-General was quite alive to the advantage arising to the public from the invention and that no steps would be taken to stop it. This 1880 judgment really began the connection of the Post Office with the telephones. Its logical outcome, one would have thought, was for the Postmaster-General to take over the telephones forthwith and develop them as a national service in close connection with the State telegraphs. But the Government of the day did not care to extend the field of State activities, which they felt should supplement rather than supersede private enterprise, though they had at the same time a nervous feeling about the possible growth of a vast monopoly which would eventually have to be purchased at enormous cost.

So they adopted a policy aimed, it would seem, at repressing the new service rather than encouraging it, and this went on with incidental disputes and troubles of various kinds until 1912 when the inevitable happened and the telephones became a State service. The actual method of administration adopted was for the Postmaster-General to grant licences to the telephone companies in return for a royalty of 10 per cent on gross receipts. At the same time the Post Office maintained the right to open exchanges of its own, to the extent necessary to provide it with an effective weapon for negotiations with the companies.

Meanwhile commercial warfare was waged between the various companies. It is recorded that on one occasion two rival companies operating in Sheffield secured wayleave for the erection of a pole in a certain important position. One of the companies dug a hole to receive the pole, but when their workmen arrived next morning with the pole to put in it, they found that their rivals had got there first and planted their own pole!

At first the telephone was used almost entirely by business people and so for some years exchange hours corresponded with normal business hours; there was no service on holidays or Sundays and of course no night service. The first all-night service in London was introduced at the United Telephone Company's Heddon Street and Westminster Exchanges in 1885, and was intended specially for the use of Members of Parliament.

The "telephone girl" did not make her appearance for some years and she did not replace the boy operators to any great extent until 1889. Some years earlier, however, the *Pall Mall Gazette*, describing a visit to an exchange in the City said:

Below the roof, in the attic, is a room occupied by eleven young ladies.... The alert dexterity with which, at the signal given by the fall of a small lid about the size of a teaspoon, the lady hitches on the applicant to the number with which he desires to talk is pleasant to watch. On the day of our visit there had been in this one office no less than 2,400 calls. Here, indeed, is an occupation to which no "heavy father" could object; and the result is that a higher class of young women can be obtained for the secluded career of a telephonist as compared with that which follows the more barmaid-like occupation of a telegraph clerk.

Many years of research and experiment were to pass before the engineers perfected a system of underground telephone circuits, and in the meantime the vicinity of a busy exchange began to look like a spider's web. Overhead lines massed together were of course very vulnerable in case of storms. A great snowstorm in London on Christmas Day, 1886, was the first serious indication of this vulnerability. It brought down most of the overhead wires in London and all the standards and poles which supported them; it cost the United Telephone Company £30,000 and the service was dislocated for several weeks. Havoc wrought by gales is still the nightmare of the Engineering Department.

Fires were a specially dreaded form of breakdown in the early days of overhead congestion. In 1898 there was a serious outbreak in Heddon Street, when a massive derrick, carrying a large number of wires and rubber-covered cables, was hurled into the street as the roof collapsed and lay there for some days, a tangled mass of ironwork, wire and cable. Other fires which followed within the next few years showed the need for an energetic policy of underground distribution. This was pursued under formidable difficulties and with much litigation with the Commissioners of Sewers and other authorities.

It is interesting to recall that the origin of all our present-day systems of underground conductors was an experiment made by Sir Francis Ronalds in 1816. Seventy years later Sir William Preece said, "It is perfectly astonishing how that man's instinct saw the various troubles that were likely to be met with in the construction of long underground lines."

The National Telephone Company was formed in 1881 for the express purpose of developing a telephone service in Scotland, and when in due course of time it became recognised that the existence of several different systems was wasteful and confusing, and an amalgamation of certain interests was carried out, it was the National which gave its name to the new organisation. The amalgamation took place on May 1, 1889, with a capital of £4 million. The Government objected to the proposal but they were outwitted. At the time of this important move a total of 23,585 lines came under the control of the National Telephone Company.

This amalgamation did not put an end to competition. But gradually the National swallowed up the minor companies until, in 1894, it had established what was practically a monopoly, since the Post Office was now the only competitor, and a competitor, moreover, which still had its hands tied by timidity over State enterprise. At the end of 1894 the National Telephone Company controlled over 73,000 lines and the Post Office between 5,000 and 6,000.

The company itself, however, by no means had its hands free. As its system grew it was handicapped more and more by its lack of wayleave powers. The Government, still adhering to a policy which was projected no further than the protection of the telegraphs, had consistently refused to delegate the powers held by the Postmaster-General under the Telegraph Acts, to place poles or lay underground lines in public roads or along the railways, and the company was therefore obliged without help to drive hard bargains, often at exorbitant rates, with landowners and public authorities.

It was largely the force of public complaint at the service provided that led the Government at last to change its policy. In 1896 the trunk system passed to the control of the Post Office, the purchase price being £459,000. This seemed to intensify the troubles of the company. It began to be appreciated that a State-owned system would not be such a terrible danger after all. An influential agitation sprang up in favour of Government purchase of the whole system. There followed a further period of difficulty and discord during which the Post Office introduced a service of its own in the London area, partly supplementing and partly in competition with the National Telephone Company's system. Several municipalities also set up telephone systems of their own. At last, in 1905, an agreement was reached under which the Government acquired the option of taking over the whole of the company's service at the end of 1911, at the value of the plant. At midnight on December 31, 1911, all the assets of the company passed into the hands of the Postmaster-General at a price subsequently, after much arbitration, fixed at just under £12,500,000, which from the taxpayer's point of view compared very favourably with the company's original claim of nearly £21 million.

On January 1, 1912, the Post Office at last found itself in full control of the telephone service of the country, except for two surviving municipal systems, owned by the Corporations of Hull and Portsmouth. The Portsmouth system was merged in the Post Office in 1913, but Hull still remains outside the Post Office system and is run by the municipality. The Channel Islands system is also independent of the Post Office.

The department at once bent itself to the task of merging the telephone system into the General Post Office organisation in order that it should become part of the great national system of communications directed from St Martin's-le-Grand. The National Telephone Company's employees, numbering 19,000, were absorbed; a beginning was made at the combination of the separate trunk and local exchanges; a vigorous policy of installing underground cable systems in substitution for the overhead systems was inaugurated; and a notable amount of energy was devoted to the extension of the telephone service into rural areas which had not hitherto enjoyed it. In the two and a half years which elapsed before War broke out 450 villages in various parts of the country had been given exchanges. From that time up to the present it has been the consistent policy of the Post Office to extend telephone facilities, and indeed communication facilities of all sorts, into the country districts, so that a really national system, regardless of sectional losses, has been established.

But the most formidable task which confronted the Post Office, and especially its engineers, at the transfer, was that of bringing the ordinary exchange equipment up-to-date. Naturally enough, during the six years that passed between the signing of the transfer agreement and the transfer itself, the National Telephone Company had not been inclined to dip its hand deeply into its pocket for the expenditure of capital, especially as the agreement made no particular provision to force it to do so. Consequently the new owners found themselves faced with much antiquated plant and with little margin of spare wires or switchboard accommodation. A good deal had been done by 1914 to amalgamate the two systems and replace obsolete plant, but there were still heavy arrears to be overtaken when the outbreak of war brought the process to a standstill.

The home telephone service had to take its chance while the demands of the fighting forces were satisfied and naturally no one grumbled much at the time; that was to come later. At the moment the services of the highly skilled men of the department were indispensable elsewhere; first and last some 13,000 men, more than half the staff of the Engineering Department, were diverted entirely to war service. A large number of the expert female operators also left the service in order to do work more important in the national emergency. Their places were filled by inexperienced girls or boys, who had to be trained not only to the needs of a normal service but also to the many needs of the naval, military and air forces. In connection with air raids, and in many other respects, the telephone system became a vital portion of "Home Defence" and military organisation generally, and the girl operators were frequently called upon to carry on to the accompaniment of exploding bombs and anti-aircraft barrage. They did so with splendid gallantry.

Coming down to the present time, we find the inland telephone service in a state of active development and rapid change. The principal feature of this development is the introduction of the automatic system, which did not get seriously under way until 1923. To-day there are some 2,500 automatic exchanges, and additional conversions from manual working are taking place very rapidly. The total number of telephones now working automatically is roughly 1,500,000, or 50 per cent of the whole.

The complications and difficulties which attend the conversion of a telephone area from manual to automatic working vary with the density of the population, and the most difficult problem of all is the conversion now taking place of the whole London system within a 12½ miles radius of Oxford Circus, so as to form an inter-working self-contained automatic system.

For administrative purposes the London Telephone Region covers an area of approximately 1,200 square miles and extends from Welwyn in the north to Reigate in the south and from Staines in the west to Gravesend in the east. It has been found that the best results are obtained by grouping subscribers on exchange centres in such a way that the length of any subscriber's line does not as a rule exceed two miles; at the same time no exchange grouping must contain more than 9,999 lines. As a result of these physical limitations, and economic limitations as well, it has been found necessary to provide over 250 exchanges in the London Region.

The task of the administration is to ensure that any subscriber in the whole of the London Area can obtain immediate connection to any other subscriber in the area by the simplest possible process. To this end it has been necessary to provide and maintain a most complicated spider's web of earthenware, lead and copper, linking up all the exchanges either directly with one another or in some cases through connecting centres.

Although nearly 70 per cent of the calls originated in London are made by subscribers on automatic exchanges a large operating staff is still necessary. In London's local exchanges alone there are between six and seven thousand operators employed during the ordinary day hours and some 2,000 men for handling the late evening and night traffic, while the handling of trunk calls requires the employment of nearly 1,400 day operators in addition.

Indeed, taking the country as a whole, in spite of the progressive mechanisation of the telephones, the number of staff directly employed by the Post Office services as a

Manual telephone exchange, Birmingham

whole goes on steadily rising. As to the amount of employment given *indirectly* by the Post Office telephone system it is difficult to make even a guess, for it provides work for men, not only in domestic industries, but in mines and factories all over the country and in distant parts of the world. More than 50 trades are intimately concerned in it, among them being makers of exchange equipment, cable makers, instrument makers, copper-wire drawers, battery makers, earthenware-duct makers, road contractors, as well as the people who make insulating paper, rubber and varnishes, the industries which make screws, fibre, cotton, silk yarn; and the miners who produce copper, iron, lead, tin, zinc, nickel, silver, mica, gold and platinum.

The continuous growth in the number of telephone subscribers, coupled with the physical limitations of an exchange, creates from time to time the need for new exchanges not only on the outer rim of an area but in the centre of it. This involves re-arrangement of exchange areas and, unfortunately, the alteration of a large number of subscribers' numbers. Some subscribers raise difficulties over this and are not easily satisfied of its necessity, but on the whole the public co-operate cheerfully.

In some cases subscribers show a special fondness for telephone numbers to which they have grown accustomed. Others are still superstitious and rather dread a telephone number which they can show in any way to have some relation to the mystic number "13". The fondness for a number is sometimes due to the fact that a particular grouping of digits has a ring to it or the arrangement is one which can easily be remembered. In one instance a lady deplored the proposal to change her number 3015 as she said her family were tennis enthusiasts and 3015 was always remembered readily. Fortunately it was possible to offer 4030, and this number was at once accepted.

Another subscriber was not so amenable. The visiting official in his most engaging manner offered him 1066 which he suggested was easily remembered as the date of William the Conqueror. "Have you got 1665?" he was asked. He had, and he enquired the reason for its selection. "More appropriate to the service you represent! That was the year of the Great Plague!"

It is not always possible, for technical reasons, to give a new exchange in the London area, or any other area where letters have to be dialled as well as figures, the name of the district in which the exchange is situated. There cannot, for instance, be both HAMpstead and HAMmersmith—or even both HOLborn and GOLdersgreen, because dialling GOL would produce the same result as dialling HOL. Nor can any exchange name begin with O, because dialling that letter the subscriber is automatically put through to an operator. It has therefore been necessary to depart in some cases from the use of well-known local names. Local authorities are consulted when some arbitrary name is involved and as far as possible their preferences are acted upon. Thus Hammersmith became "Riverside", an alternative which no doubt cheered the heart of Mr A. P. Herbert; and Golder's Green became "Speedwell".

Many alternatives are sometimes considered before one of these arbitrary names is decided upon. The authorities have to be particularly careful not to offend local susceptibilities; "Deepwater" was the picturesque name first suggested for an exchange in the City but it was felt that financiers might not appreciate it and the suggestion was dropped.

The names of famous men are specially favoured by the Telephone Department and these generally find favour locally as well. Battersea has a "Macaulay" exchange because the historian lived close by. A Chelsea exchange is called "Flaxman" after the sculptor, and

Twickenham acquired "Popesgrove", commemorating the poet; at these exchanges relics of the great men they commemorate have been accumulated, and Pope, at least, who, one seems to recall, was not too proud of his villa at Twickenham, would no doubt be soothed by this tribute. A similar fancy gives Harrow a "Byron" exchange, though the dialling of BYR is perhaps a shade too reminiscent of a French *apéritif*.

Except in the largest cities it is not necessary to install this "Director" system; the needs of other towns can be met by a less-complex system involving the use of numbers only, without the initial letters of the name of the exchange.

The introduction of automatic working has been a great boon to the rural districts, for by this means a continuous service has been given in areas where the cost of a manually operated equipment would have been, in relation to the number of subscribers to be served, quite prohibitive.

The requirements of the countryman have been still further met, during the past year or two, by a wide extension of call office facilities. To-day even the most remote hamlet, too small to possess a post office, can have its telephone kiosk, and if the amount of traffic does not justify it by ordinary standards, the Postmaster-General will have one installed on the application of the local parish council, provided the council is willing to pay for five years the rental of one ordinary private telephone line—£4 per annum. What this development means to the amenities of life in the country can be easily realised, and in placing the farmer in instant touch with his market it is also proving a considerable boon to agriculture.

Side by side with the development of automatic working for the completion of local calls a remodelling of the trunk service of the country has been proceeding. Until a comparatively short time ago a subscriber wishing to make a trunk call had to book his call with an operator and then, replacing his receiver, wait until the operator had matured the call and summoned him to the receiver again. This tiresome procedure has been abolished; the caller is now placed directly in connection with a trunk operator who is generally able to complete the desired call while the caller waits at the telephone. Only rarely now is the subscriber asked to replace his receiver and wait to be called again.

This radical change in practice naturally involved an enormous amount of engineering and structural work; trunk exchanges throughout the country had to be rebuilt, a far-reaching reorganisation of the trunk network had to be undertaken and entirely new methods of operation had to be adopted. In due course, however, the task was completed and a normal trunk call has lost all its ancient terrors. At night time, owing to the rush of business following the reduction of rates after seven o'clock, some delay on certain lines, especially those bearing summer holiday traffic, is still experienced. It would be uneconomic to provide a "no-delay" service to meet this short, seasonal rush and in time no doubt the peak will flatten itself out.

There are many exchanges throughout the country which deal solely with the connection of long-distance calls, but of all these the trunk exchange in London, which occupies part of the Faraday Building, in Queen Victoria Street, is by far the largest. It is made up of seven separate switchrooms occupying four floors of the building. All these rooms operate as one exchange. About 3,200 trunk calls are originated during a busy hour, and during the cheap night-rate period over 8,000 are handled. During the daytime 85 per cent of the trunk calls are put through within 90 seconds.

The operator receives notice of a trunk call by the glowing of a lamp, and she at once passes the call forward, either direct to the exchange called or to an intermediate exchange, by connection to the required trunk circuit. She has the additional task of timing the calls. As soon as the call is put through and the two persons connected begin to speak, the operator switches into action an automatic timing apparatus. When each period of three minutes has nearly elapsed (actually twelve seconds are allowed for the final farewells), an automatic time signal consisting of three " pips" is sent out as a warning of the passage of time. Until recently the operator herself had to break into the conversation to utter the warning but the mechanical innovation is a great improvement. When the caller replaces his receiver, he stops the timing apparatus and the duration of the call is automatically displayed to the operator, who enters particulars on a small paper ticket, one end of which is bent up to form an ingenious "sail". With the aid of this contrivance it is wafted through a pneumatic tube to a central point where it is sorted with others and despatched to the accounts branch to be included in the account, which in turn reaches the subscriber with an infallible regularity which is only in keeping with the rest of the system.

The future development of the trunk system will be in the direction of mechanisation. It is not intended to mechanise it entirely, because it is recognised that the supervision and assistance of an operator will always be more in demand than on the simpler short distance calls. At present, however, the setting up of a long-distance call may require the services of two, three, or even more operators, and the next step will be to achieve greater speed in working by the substitution of automatic switching apparatus for at any rate some of the operators. The ideal aimed at, which may take some considerable time to realise, is that any trunk call will require the services of one operator only for supervision and assistance, all intermediate switching being performed automatically.

Also housed in Faraday Building is the London Toll Exchange. The metropolitan area has especially close business and social associations with the provincial areas within a radius of 60 to 70 miles from the centre, and it is to secure a specially high standard of service within this area that the separate system of junction lines known as the Toll System has been organised.

The calls to places in this toll area are controlled by groups of operators stationed in the various local exchanges at special switchboards, and the whole of the area is served by groups of lines which radiate from Faraday Building. Over 200,000 toll calls are dealt with here each day. It was the success of the policy of providing calls to places in the toll area "on demand" that led, after considerable experience, to the solution of the problem of providing calls on demand to all places in the United Kingdom.

Faraday Building is not only the centre of the London Telephone Service. It is also the home of the International Exchange, which has been aptly called "the world's switchboard". First, there is the Continental Exchange where, by means of 165 direct circuits by underground wires and submarine cables, operators can connect any telephone "subscriber" (as the renter of a telephone is still quaintly called) in this country with Paris or Moscow or Berlin or Rome, or practically any place in Europe, as easily as a trunk operator could put a Londoner through to Birmingham or Bristol. The operators here—or at least a proportion of them—are of course accomplished linguists. Fortunately each country does not require to be called in its own tongue, and by international agreement the greater part of the necessary speech between

British and Continental operators is conducted in English, French or German. But if, as sometimes happens, Italian or Spanish has to be used the Faraday switchboard can supply the talent necessary to complete the connection. In addition the exchange provides a special staff of operators to answer all types of enquiry about the Continental Exchange system.

The Radio Terminal Station is in another part of Faraday Building. Here are the terminals of the 15 direct radiotelephone channels operated from London. The girl talking quietly into a mouthpiece before a switchboard labelled with such names as Cape Town, Sydney, New York or Tokyo—talking as quietly as she would to the girl sitting by her side—is actually in direct communication with an operator thousands of miles away.

One of the major miracles of the place is the process of voice distortion. An essential of a good telephone service is that conversation should not be overheard by someone for whom it is not intended. To secure secrecy, speech is deliberately distorted or "scrambled" before it starts on the radio part of its journey. At the other end the process is inverted and the voice is put together and made normal and intelligible again.

It is trite to say that the telephone has linked the world together in a way that our fathers never imagined. To-day this country is linked with nearly every part of the globe and it is possible to speak through one's own domestic instrument to practically all telephone subscribers in foreign countries. However much one may be inclined at the moment, after taking a look round at the international situation, to ask if the world has really progressed by all this intensified linking up, the physical fact remains as one of the marvels of this staggering century. It is in these days quite possible for a British firm in London to confer with its representatives in, say, Paris, New York, Sydney, Bombay and Cape Town simultaneously, all being linked up and in as close conversational touch as though they were sitting round the board-room table in London. It is true that they cannot at present watch each other's facial expressions, but television is already striding ahead of its infantile limitations and some day visual contact may be as possible as oral.

Although it is only a period well within a single life-time since Watson, Graham Bell's assistant, heard the words, "Mr Watson, come here! I want you!", which was the first speech heard over a telephone circuit, the number of telephones in the world is now about 35 millions, of which number 3 millions are in the United Kingdom. From these 3 million instruments some 2,000 million calls are made annually, and of these about 100 millions are long distance, or trunk calls.

Nothing could illustrate better the rapidity of telephone development than this letter from Lieut.-General Sir George Cory which was published recently in *The Times*:

Many years ago in Hamilton, Canada, my mother, Mrs C. D. Cory, then a young married woman with keen hearing and a clear voice, helped Professor Bell in his talking experiments with the very first telephone, which was used on a rough wire between some friends' houses. Shortly afterwards my father was one of the first three subscribers on the first telephone exchange. The other night I was speaking at the Wolfe Society dinner at Westerham, with a microphone on the table, and next morning I received a cable from my mother, in Canada, saying: "delighted to hear your voice." What a difference, and in one life-time, between that first strained hearing from a few hundred yards away and this last!

In passing it may be mentioned that the International Exchange has a good variety of what may be called "man-hunting" problems to cope with. It frequently happens that the individual required is not at the telephone quoted by the caller but has gone elsewhere; in such cases the operator makes every effort to find him, chasing him perhaps to another country. Recently a lady wished to speak urgently to her husband who was travelling home from Switzerland. After enquiries regarding his probable route the London staff got into touch with Paris and arranged with the stationmaster of the station at which the Swiss train was arriving for the husband to be found. This was done and facilities were given for him to talk to his wife from a telephone in the station.

This sort of research work, it may be assumed, is not exactly courted, but the incident is useful as indicating what "International" can do when it is really on its mettle.

The practical co-ordination of the long-distance telephone service in Europe naturally calls in a high degree for international co-operation. This is secured by an international advisory body called the Comité Consultatif International Téléphonique, which is usually referred to by the abbreviation "C.C.I.F." (F standing for "Fones").

This committee originated in the common desire of the European nations after the War, not only to make up leeway, but to take urgent advantage of recent scientific discoveries, and forge ahead to the accomplishment of a really efficient service of international communication. For this purpose close co-operation is essential, since to make an international call effective the systems of the terminal countries, and possibly of several intermediate countries as well, have to be temporarily linked together. As the speakers are generally of different nationalities, there would be confusion unless the quality of transmission were uniformly good; hence there must be agreement in the design and maintenance of equipment and also in operating procedure. The success of the committee in bringing about this agreement and securing a high

standard of smooth international working has been very
marked.

While the telephone becomes more and more an
essential of domestic life we still have a long way to go
before we reach the position achieved by other countries.
Comparing the number of telephones per hundred inhabitants, the United Kingdom comes only ninth in the
list of nations. According to a recent statement, the
United States heads the list with 13·7 telephones per cent
of population; Canada comes second with 11; then
follow Denmark, New Zealand, Sweden, Switzerland,
Australia, and Norway, in that order, until we get to
Great Britain with 5·4 telephones per hundred inhabitants. We reached our present position in the list by over-
taking Germany in 1933.

The main reason for the United Kingdom's low place
in this list is that, being primarily an industrial nation,
she has a large proportion of wage-earners in her population by whom a telephone is still regarded as a luxury.
Moreover, she has highly efficient postal and telegraph
services which provide rapid means of communication
within her limited boundaries.

The luxury feeling is, however, steadily diminishing,
because, while most of the necessaries of life have shown
a tendency in recent years to cost more, the cost of the
telephone has progressively decreased. The effect of the
successive tariff changes are singularly interesting. First
of all, let it be said that the guiding principle is that the
tariff should be such as to stimulate development of the
service while covering the present or future cost of providing it. This formula fortunately covers the provision
of certain sections of the service, in rural communities for
example, at less than cost price.

In 1921 a business or residential line in London cost
£8. 10s. a year; the present tariff for a business line is

£7. 2s. and for a residential line £5. 4s. with an allowance of 200 free calls a year. The intermediate reductions by which these figures were reached each brought about an immediate increase in sales, but there was something in the "free call" feature introduced in October 1936 which made a special appeal, and the rush of new clients proved that the lure of "something for nothing" had been underestimated.

The trunk call rate reductions, however, have provided the most remarkable results. When the night trunk maximum rate of 1s. for any distance was introduced in 1934, the night calls sprang up in a year by 169 per cent; the summer peak of the night traffic (during August) actually showed an increase of 193 per cent.

This altogether extraordinary increase was, of course, very welcome. It not only produced revenue but it showed that Post Office policy was making the community really "telephone minded", for it seems that the extra traffic is almost entirely social and almost wholly new. But what the rapid growth meant to engineering and operational activities may be conveyed by one significant figure. Before the introduction of the cheap night rate the number of trunk circuits between London and Scotland was 31; by the end of 1937 there were over 100.

The methods of modern publicity have been applied very freely to make the telephone popular, and behind the Publicity Department, consolidating, as it were, the ground won by the shock troops, is the sales organisation, a corps of some 900 men including in normal times 760 sales representatives, whose duty is not only to canvass for new orders but to advise and help in the use of the telephone and the other Post Office services. Within this organisation is a group constantly engaged on the forecast of development, both nationally and in individual exchange areas. Accurate forecasts of this description are essential in order that plant may be laid out in the most economical way to meet future needs and that new exchanges may be provided in positions which involve a minimum of external cabling. There is also a "Sales Investigation" group which studies methods of salesmanship and sees that they are applied to the best advantage.

Having established the principle that the telephone is an essential of modern life, the Post Office has set itself to increase the range of its usefulness. Many are probably still unaware that for a modest fee of 3d. a subscriber can be called at any time of the day or night. There was a rush on this service in the early hours of King George's Coronation Day, when people had been warned to be in their places on the route very early. The normal daily number of these alarm calls in the London area is about 3,000; it leapt on this occasion to 11,820. This particular service is not always used for the awakening of sleepers; one subscriber asked the operator to call him after the lapse of three minutes. It transpired that he was boiling an egg and his watch was out of order. In another case a busy Member of Parliament used the service to enable him to take some snatches of sleep in the intervals between a series of important engagements.

Another innovation is the Absent Subscriber service, which has recently been on trial at Liverpool; the operator, for a fee of 6d., will intercept all calls for a day, dictate and accept messages and act, in fact, as a perfect private secretary.

A telephone subscriber can ascertain by enquiry of the Supervisor-in-Charge of his exchange, whether a fog or breakdown service is in operation on the railway. Although the number of enquiries in connection with this service has shown a considerable increase since its inception, the facility appears to be little known.

The telephone is now largely used for playing chess matches. The Post Office reserves the necessary lines and has even, with the approval of the British Chess Federation, laid down the procedure.

An Enquiry Office service for London is at present in contemplation which will enable a caller, on dialling a special code, to obtain information on any matter which comes within the province of the Post Office.

Recently complaint was made that the means of summoning the police, the fire brigade or an ambulance by automatic telephone in cases of extreme urgency were not entirely effective. Major Tryon immediately appointed a committee to advise him what could be done to give this emergency service its full value to the public, and the result was the now familiar instruction to "dial 999". This signal sets a loud buzzer in action in the exchange and a red light glows as well. The operator, of course, deals with this signal without a second's delay. In the first week of this new alarm system a burglar was caught by its means and the public were quick to appreciate its advantages; "999" is admittedly not the fastest combination of figures to dial but for technical reasons no other was possible. At present the new alarm is confined to the London area, but its extension to some of the larger provincial towns is being considered. It is quite startling to find how frequently the police, the fire brigade or the ambulance service is required; during the first three months of the "999" service legitimate emergency calls in London numbered over 40,000.

The most popular of the new telephone services is that known as "TIM". On dialling these letters the caller becomes automatically connected with the Speaking Clock and is told the exact time by "The Girl with the Golden Voice". The selection of this girl, who turned out to be Miss E. W. Cain of the Victoria Exchange, was one of the brightest of the Post Office publicity efforts. After careful elimination nine operators were selected for the final test from over 15,000 in exchanges throughout England.

Mr John Masefield, Dame Sybil Thorndike, Lord Iliffe, Mr S. Hibberd, chief announcer of the B.B.C., and Mrs E. D. Atkinson were the judges, Mrs Atkinson (a sister of Mr Humbert Wolfe) having been selected by telephone operators throughout England as the perfect telephone subscriber. The Speaking Clock is to be extended to certain centres in the provinces, but whether a typically English voice like Miss Cain's will satisfy Scotland and Wales remains to be seen. And then what shall prevent Manchester or Leeds from demanding that their own Golden Voice shall tell the hour in the local vernacular?

Telephone operators may not all be Girls with Golden Voices—indeed after 8 p.m. there is a startling transition from soprano to bass or from contralto to tenor. The automatic "dialling tone" is now rapidly displacing the pleasantly intoned "Number, please?"—with its carefully graduated inflections when the number is not immediately forthcoming!—but it will be a long time before the human (and humane) operator becomes obsolete. One person who would miss them is Mr George Bernard Shaw, whose authority in telephone matters has already been mentioned. Recently in the course of a criticism of speech on the modern stage he said, by way of contrast, "the telephone girls are wonderful: they speak so clearly that they are not only efficient but peremptory and terrifying".

More than one tragedy has been averted by the quick action of an operator—for instance, in summoning a doctor when it is obvious that the caller is in distress. One girl, answering a call, found a nursemaid almost hysterical with fear because the child of whom she was in sole charge was in a fit. The operator advised her to put the child into a warm bath, took the caller's address and rang up a doctor who was promptly on the scene. A little later the mother of the child rang up the exchange to express her gratitude.

International Telephone Exchange, London

In another case a night operator received a signal and on answering with "Number, please?" heard nothing but a dog barking. The operator listened for some seconds—the dog continued to bark and growl and a scuffling noise was heard as if a struggle was taking place. The operator quickly looked up the subscriber's name and address, told the local police what he had heard and was assured that they would at once send a constable round. Later, the exchange was informed that, doubtless bored by being left alone in the house, the dog had knocked the telephone over and when the police arrived was happily playing with it!

In telephones, as in agriculture, we gain a lot, no doubt, from mechanisation, but possibly we lose something as well!

CHAPTER 7

THE TALE OF THE TELEGRAPHS

The Telegraph is the father of the Telephone but, as sometimes happens, the offspring has leapt ahead in popularity and has put the aged parent somewhat in the shade. However, as this story will show, there is no sign that the parent's day is over; on the contrary, after a period of depression, he shows signs of renewed vitality.

The need for long-distance signalling naturally became apparent at a very early stage in the development of human intelligence. Signals made by breaking columns of smoke, by the tapping of drums—the bush telegraph of Africa—are of great antiquity. Herodotus, who has already been quoted as a critic of postal matters, tells how the flash of sunshine upon shields—probably the first heliograph—was used for the purpose of signalling at the Battle of Marathon, 490 B.C. But jumping from Herodotus to Shakespeare, when Puck told Oberon in 1594 that he would "put a girdle round about the earth in forty minutes", his author may, or may not, have had in mind the announcement in 1558 by the Neapolitan philosopher, Baptista Porta, that "owing to the convenience afforded by the magnet, persons can converse together through long distances", or even of his more specific statement 30 years later: "I do not fear that with a long absent friend, even though he be confined by prison walls, we can communicate what we wish by means of two compass needles circumscribed with an alphabet." The probability is, indeed, that Will Shakespeare had never even heard of Baptista Porta and that Puck's prophecy was just a brilliant flight of fancy.

For practical purposes the tale of the telegraph begins with the optical telegraph, a clumsy device consisting only of a semaphore, not unlike a railway signal, but capable of transmitting messages with astonishing rapidity. It came from France in 1790, the invention of a M. Claude Chappe, who, while studying for the Church, found himself in a seminary at Angers unhappily cut off from two brothers who lived a mile or so away. After experimenting unsuccessfully with electricity as a means of communication, he contrived this optical device in order to keep in touch with them. It inspired one of Charles Dibdin's jingles which started thus:

> If you'll only just promise you'll none of you laugh,
> I'll be after explaining the French Télégraphe!
> A machine that's endowed with such wonderful power,
> It writes, reads and sends news fifty miles in an hour.

Later stanzas went on to point out how useful the telegraph poles would be as lightning conductors and as props for clothes lines on which one could dry one's shirts.

Napoleon, seeing immediately the military usefulness of this appliance, proceeded to set up 530 observation stations covering 3,000 miles of vision, and the Russians quickly followed with a route from St Petersburg to Kronstadt. In this military use of optical telegraphs we have the beginning of State ownership, based on the principle that it was not safe to allow so important a device to be in private hands. Several routes were equipped in England and this explains the frequency of "Telegraph Hill" on the ordnance maps. It was such a "télégraphe" that brought the first news of the Battle of Trafalgar from Portsmouth to London.

But nearly 40 years before this the idea of a practical electric telegraph had been born in a letter published in the *Scots' Magazine* of February 17, 1753. It was written from Renfrew and signed with the initials "C. M." and to this day the writer of this epoch-making document has not been identified in spite of a considerable amount of speculation and research. "C. M." suggested a set of parallel wires, one for each letter of the alphabet, and a current of electricity to pick out the letters in the order desired.

New ideas, fresh developments, in the infant science are spread over the next 60 years, inscribing in telegraph history the names of Galvani and Volta, Le Sage, Lomond, Chappe, Reusser, Francisco Salva of Barcelona —the first to apply electricity dynamically for purposes of telegraphy—Alexandre—another notable pioneer and said to be the natural son of Jean-Jacques Rousseau— Ralph Wedgwood of the famous pottery family, names which in themselves indicate the geographical range of the research which was going on.

In 1816 came the experiments of Sir Francis Ronalds. "The result seemed to be", he reports in his *Descriptions of an Electrical Telegraph etc.*, published in 1823,

that that most extraordinary fluid or agency, electricity, may actually be employed for a more practically useful purpose than the gratification of the philosopher's inquisitive research, the schoolboy's idle amusement, or the physician's tool; that it may be compelled to travel as many hundred miles beneath our feet as the subterranean ghost which nightly haunts our metropolis, our provincial towns, and even our high roads; and that in such an enlightened country and obscure climate as this its travels would be productive of, at the least, as much public and private benefit. Why has no serious trial yet been made of the qualifications of so diligent a courier? And if he should be proved competent to the task, why should not our kings hold councils at Brighton with their ministers in London? Why should not our government govern at Portsmouth almost as promptly as in Downing Street? Why should our defaulters escape by default of our foggy climate? And since our piteous inamorati are not all Alphei, why should they add to the torments of absence those dilatory tormentors, pens, ink, paper, and posts? Let us have electrical conversazione offices, communicating with each other all over the kingdom, if we can.

In the same book, now very rare, Ronalds reports how his discovery was rejected by the Admiralty on the grounds that the end of the French war had made telegraphs of any kind totally unnecessary. "I felt very little disappointment", Ronalds writes, "and not a shadow of resentment on the occasion, because every one knows, that telegraphs have long been great bores at the Admiralty. Should they again become necessary, however, perhaps electricity and electricians may be indulged by his Lordship and Mr Barrow with an opportunity of proving what they are capable of in this way. I claim no indulgence for mere chimeras and chimera framers, and I hope to escape the fate of being ranked in that unenviable class."

It was a probable knowledge of Ronalds's experiments that prompted Andrew Crane to prophesy in 1816 that "by means of the electric agency we shall be enabled to communicate our thoughts instantaneously with the uttermost ends of the earth". Thus it took over 200 years to eliminate, in the realms of prophecy, that "time lag" of forty minutes imposed by Puck in *A Midsummer Night's Dream*. In the realm of practice it was another half century before our thoughts could be transmitted instantaneously even as far as America.

Another twenty years of experiment by many hands in many lands. A vital discovery by Oersted giving fresh impetus to such philosophers as Ampère, Arago, Faraday, Schweigger, De la Rive, Ohm and Henry, spectacular progress by Baron Schilling (primarily interested in electricity for its lethal possibilities), Gauss and Weber, Steinheil and Edward Davy. And at last we come to William Fothergill Cooke and Charles Wheatstone who jointly patented in 1837 a practicable system which was successfully tested over lines between Euston and Camden Town railway stations.

The partnership between Cooke and Wheatstone led to an acrimonious dispute for the honour and glory of being the inventor of the first practical telegraph system, and to a clever arbitration by Brunell and Daniell, which, while it appeared to settle the subject by dividing the honours, was not sufficiently conclusive entirely to settle the dispute. Each partner wrote a pamphlet on the subject. "He demands indeed", wrote Wheatstone in reply to Cooke, "to be the first of telegraphic inventors, and the Award allows him to be the first of *undertakers*; and he cannot see, or prefers not to see, the distinction."

It is a curious fact, not unearthed till long afterwards, that Dr Edward Davy, who practised as a dispensing chemist in the Strand, had invented in 1836 a telegraphic system as important as Wheatstone's. "It is certain", says Mr J. J. Fahie, who discovered Edward Davy and his work nearly 50 years later, "that he had a clearer grasp of the requirements and capabilities of an electric telegraph than, probably, Cooke and Wheatstone themselves; and had he been taken up by capitalists, and his idea licked into shape by actual practice, as they and theirs were, he would have successfully competed with them for a share of the profits and honours which have so largely accrued to them as the practical introducers of the electric telegraph." Instead, having opposed the grant of a patent to Cooke and Wheatstone, he left the country and lived for many years afterwards in Australia; shortly after he left, his father sold his invention for £600. Incidentally here is a singularly interesting and prophetic extract from a letter which Davy wrote on the subject of telegraphy to his father in 1838: "I think our Government ought, and perhaps will, eventually take it upon themselves as a branch of the Post Office; yet I can scarcely imagine that there would be such absurd illiberality as to prohibit or appropriate it without compensation."

The story of Edward Davy is, however, mentioned here only as a romantic sidelight on the introduction of telegraphy. Cooke and Wheatstone were in possession of the necessary rights; their experiments between Euston and Camden Town succeeded and they went ahead and prospered. Some few years later it happened that another telegraph line which had been laid along the Great Western Railway from Paddington to Slough was instrumental in bringing to justice the Quaker murderer Tarvell; this brought the new invention dramatically to public notice. It is curious how closely history repeated itself many years later when wireless telegraphy, then in its infancy, took a prominent part in the apprehension of the murderer Crippen.

Another early case of detection on the Paddington-Slough railway is tersely described in an old Paddington record of telegraph messages:

Paddington, 10.50 a.m.—Special train just left. It contained two thieves: one named Oliver Martin, who is dressed in black, crape on his hat; the other named Fiddler Dick, in black trousers and light blouse. Both in the third compartment of the first second-class carriage.

Slough, 11.16 a.m.—Special train arrived. Officers have taken the two thieves into custody, a lady having lost her bag, containing a purse with two sovereigns and some silver in it; one of the sovereigns was sworn to by the lady as having been her property. It was found in Fiddler Dick's watch-fob.

The coming of the railways had a very stimulating effect upon telegraph progress because it made possible for the first time practical experiments between points actually distant from each other; demonstrations over such a course could be much more convincing than over ten miles of wire running round an inventor's garden. So practical electric telegraphy was, as we have seen, born beside a railway; round the railways the system grew up, and the railway companies used it for their own signalling purposes for some ten years before its advantages were thrown open to the public.

Then several private telegraph companies came on the scene, confining their operations strictly to those places where there was sufficient traffic to make business profitable.

Charles Dickens described the operations of one of these private bodies, the London District Telegraph Company, Ltd., in *All the Year Round*:

One hundred and sixty miles of wire are now fixed along parapets, through trees, over garrets, round chimney-pots, and across roads on the southern side of the river, and the other one hundred and twenty required miles will soon be fixed in the same manner on the northern side. The difficulty decreases as the work goes on, and the sturdiest Englishman is ready to give up the roof of his castle in the interests of science and the public good, when he finds that many hundreds of his neighbours have already led the way.

The outdoor mechanical engineers of this London district telegraph require at least six house-top resting-places in the space of a mile. To get these places at the nominal rent of a shilling a year (with three months' notice for removal) has been the object of the Company, professedly that a low tariff of charges may be based upon a moderate outlay of capital on the permanent way. The peculiarity of the company's operations, in appealing rather to the public sentiment of the middle and lower classes than to their sense of business or desire for gain, has prolonged its outdoor negotiations; but not to any great extent. The trial may have been severe, but the British householder, with a few exceptions, has nobly stood the test. He has shown that, if properly applied to and properly treated, he may belong to a nation of shopkeepers, and yet be something more than a mere mercenary citizen.

This gives a fair picture of what went on in the large towns, where each company had an office and there was a considerable amount of wasteful competition. This competition, however, had one good effect; it kept rates down, and it is a little astonishing to find rates at that time as low as 1s. for 20 words, excluding the names and addresses of sender and addressee, which were tele-graphed free of charge. For the longer distances within the limits of Great Britain the rate certainly was as high as 2s. for 20 words, and to Ireland a message of similar length cost 6s., but even these charges do not seem high when one considers the heavy capital cost involved in setting the service on its feet.

Naturally complaints soon began to be heard from the smaller towns and rural areas which were omitted from a system run essentially for the benefit of the shareholders, and demand for State ownership arose. There were many complaints about the companies' system apart from its exclusiveness; the operating was indifferent and there were frequent inaccuracies; delays were often serious; and the differential tariff was disliked. So it came about that by two Acts, in 1868 and 1869, the Government of the day, Disraeli being Prime Minister, took power to purchase the inland telegraph system and gave the Postmaster-General a monopoly of the business.

This monopoly is extremely comprehensive and indeed, remembering the similar powers enjoyed over the mail services, it is difficult to think of any form of communica-tion, unless it be imbedded in a parcel sent by rail or private carrier, to which the monopoly does not extend. We have already seen the dismay caused among private telephone interests when the High Court decided that a telephone was a telegraph, within the meaning of the Acts. But, further than this, a telegraph is held to mean "a wire or wires used for the purpose of telegraphic communication, whether worked by electricity or not, and any apparatus connected therewith, and also any apparatus for transmitting messages or other communications by means of electric signals, whether involving the use of wires or not". Fire-alarm circuits are telegraphs and even signals conveyed by means of bells worked by wires pulled by hand come legally under this description. In fact the small boy's toy telephone across the street is an infringement of the Postmaster-General's monopoly, a fact which, if he only knew it, would add vastly to his enjoyment of its somewhat elementary amenities.

The total capital expenditure involved by the transfer of the telegraphs to the State under the legislation of 1870 was a little over £10,000,000. Of this £7,200,000 went in compensation to the telegraph companies and £800,000 to the railways. Over £2,000,000 in addition were spent by the Post Office within three or four years on the extensions and improvements for which there was loud public demand. Consols were issued in 1873 to cover the total cost, which thus became merged in the National Debt, and the money for all subsequent developments of the service has been voted by Parliament with other moneys required for Post Office purposes.

The tariff was revised directly the transfer was made. The old minimum of 1s. for 20 words or less was retained, with an additional 3d. for every extra five words, the name and address of sender and addressee being still sent free, but the charge was made irrespective of the distance to be covered, which was, of course, a very great boon. The extension of the new service was at once put in hand and in three years 2,500 new postal telegraph offices had been opened and the number of messages dealt with had risen from 7 millions to 15 millions annually.

In its solicitude for the rural areas the Post Office has always acted consistently with the tradition which it set up on this occasion, and as a result our village communities are indulged to an extent not usual in other countries.

Traffic during the first decade of Post Office control mounted steadily until it began to appear that the service might one day pay for itself, but in 1883 these bright financial prospects suffered a severe check. A private member moved a resolution in the House of Commons that the time had arrived when the minimum charge for an ordinary telegram should be reduced to 6d. Against the advice of the Government the resolution was carried, and though Ministers realised that the reduction would mean both a heavy loss of revenue and a serious increase in capital expenditure, they decided to accept the decision of the House. Possibly no private member's motion before or since has had such a devastating effect upon public finance or such a beneficial effect upon public amenities. In introducing the new tariff the Postmaster-General seized the opportunity to abolish the free transmission of the name and address of the sender and the recipient, but in spite of this a swift and embarrassing increase of traffic took place; the number of telegrams of all sorts arose from 33 millions to 50 millions in two years, a jump of over 50 per cent. From this time onwards the telegraph became a very important factor in the social life of the community. The tempo of existence was speeded up, just as it was to be speeded up again later on by the internal combustion engine. One remarkable illustration of this was afforded in the elections of 1906 when Mr Balfour's sensational defeat at Manchester was used to affect other elections and undoubtedly succeeded in so doing. One of the apologists said afterwards that had there been no telegraph the tide could have been stemmed.

The sixpenny telegram lasted without interruption until 1915, when the minimum charge was raised to 9d. Nothing short of the exigencies of war could have brought this change about, for the man-in-the-street had become curiously proud of the "sixpenny" in spite of, perhaps because of, its uneconomic basis.

In 1920, owing to the heavy increase in the cost of labour and material, further increases in the tariff for inland telegrams were decided upon. The minimum charge was then fixed at 1s. for 12 words and 1d. for each additional word, and the traffic began to fall steeply.

As a result mainly of the competition of the telephone, the use of the telegram steadily declined from the high-water mark of 82 million telegrams which had been reached in 1919 to the low-water mark of 35,250,000 in 1934. A committee under the chairmanship of Sir Hardman Lever had enquired into the whole position in 1927; this committee inspired valuable work in many directions, but no action was taken on its very tentative recommendation that the charge to the public should be increased. Instead, a policy of reducing costs was actively followed and the financial position was somewhat improved; but the decline in traffic continued.

A Departmental Committee considered the situation again in 1934, and took the bold step of recommending the restoration of the sixpenny telegram. It was not quite the old pre-war sixpenny telegram: the minimum of 6d. covered nine words instead of twelve, and the charge for each subsequent word was 1d. instead of ½d. But it was as near an approach to the pre-war telegram as the financial position permitted. It contained at any rate the magic element of "sixpence".

The reduction was inaugurated by the Duke of Windsor,

then Prince of Wales, in 1935, as one of the concessions in honour of King George's Jubilee; the occasion marked the golden jubilee of the original sixpenny telegram of 1885. The public reaction to the new rate was immediately favourable; and the first year showed an increase of about 9 millions of messages.

The "Greetings Telegram", which is increasing in popularity as it becomes more widely known, was introduced on July 24, 1935. Its introduction was a veritable inspiration. On payment of an extra charge of 3d., the sender may have his telegram of greetings delivered on a special festive form, enclosed in a golden envelope. It at once became evident that the service met a real public need. Nearly 25,000 messages were sent in the first week, and within a year this figure was more than doubled. 60,000 greetings telegrams are now sent every week; they represent over 8 per cent of the total inland telegram traffic. An examination shows that about 57 per cent of these greetings messages are sent in connection with birthdays and about 10 per cent in connection with weddings.

New greetings forms are introduced from time to time but the golden envelope remains. A specially interesting innovation in connection with the greetings telegram was the issue of a special form for St Valentine's Day, 1936; although its use was confined to a single day, nearly 50,000 of these telegrams were sent, and the success was repeated in subsequent years. St Valentine had for many years been on the shelf; no one ever thought of him; it was left to St Martin's-le-Grand to bring him down and put him as it were into the window, and it now looks as if this once popular saint is in for a new lease of life. These Valentine telegrams, by the way, frequently run to considerable length and are often in verse. One effusion ended thus,

> And now I've asked you to be mine—
> By gosh! it's cost me eight and nine!

The greetings telegram is not only a "good line" in itself: it also gives the telegraph service a chance to play its part in the joyful occasions of life, and helps to dispel that atmosphere of dread and sorrow with which the telegram was so often surrounded in the past. Many people have the most ordinary messages sent as greetings telegrams simply to ensure that the recipient shall not have even a momentary anxiety when the telegram arrives.

A few more bright ideas of this kind for the purpose of encouraging and stimulating the telegraph habit would be welcomed, but it is unlikely that the telegraph service will ever be remunerative. What is much more likely is that there will be an increasing tendency to consider telegraphs and telephones as one service, as they already are by Act of Parliament, and to regard it as right and proper that "what is lost on the swings is gained on the roundabouts". Already for administrative purposes the two services are linked in the somewhat-terrifying word "Telecommunications". The rapidly growing telephone system, and especially its expanding facilities for long-distance conversation, naturally make serious inroads into telegraph traffic.

Still, as the finances of the two services are at present kept distinct, it may as well be placed on record that though the telegraphs have never paid their way, the latest figures available show a deficit of about £700,000 for the year. This figure, though high, compares well with the £1,300,000 which represented the deficit ten years ago. The improvement has been achieved mainly by strenuous efforts to reduce costs, by constant review of practice, and unremitting research on the engineering side.

The Lever Committee of 1927 and the Departmental Commission which visited the United States in 1928 were responsible for a good many improvements. Important recommendations regarding the layout and equipment of telegraph instrument rooms, staffing arrangements affecting the allocation of work, rate of working, specialisation of duties and recruitment, have been adopted with success.

But the introduction of the Teleprinter has revolutionised the service more than anything. In substitution for the old Morse signalling either by the hand-key or by the Wheatstone transmitter, which necessitated long technical training and a high degree of manipulative skill, there appeared in 1922 from America this simple-looking instrument with a typewriter keyboard, working direct to the line at the speed of roughly double that of a Morse sounder circuit, and at the other end of the line printing the telegram ready for delivery. Its advantages were manifest, and experiments for the next few years by the Post Office Engineers made it eventually possible to adopt a British-made teleprinter.

By 1934 practically the whole of the telegraph circuits in the country had been converted to teleprinter operation. Teleprinter working to the Continent is also being introduced whenever circumstances permit and it is already in operation to Holland, Belgium and Switzerland.

The actual handling of a telegram by the Post Office is worth watching. Elaborate safeguards are prescribed for the protection not only of the public but also of the employees. First of all the greatest care is taken to ensure absolute secrecy; every official, down to the messenger, employed in dealing with telegrams is required to give an undertaking that he will never divulge the contents of a message, except under subpoena in a court of law; any breach of this undertaking renders him liable to imprisonment.

Great care is also exercised in the prevention of forgery or fraudulent alteration in telegrams. The Post Office, for instance, has to guard against the small, and happily decreasing, number of people who from time to time endeavour to back the winner of a race after the horses have passed the post. It is now extremely difficult to defraud the bookie in this way.

The counter clerk, having accepted and timed the telegram, affixes postage stamps to represent the cost; in times gone by the sender had to do this for himself. Next, a serial number is entered on the form and the telegram is placed in a chute or tube carrier for convey-ance to the instrument room. This ends the responsibility of the counter clerk, but this description of his essential duties does scant justice to the extensive range of know-ledge and sympathy which is expected from him by the public. He must be able to answer, so far as is humanly possible, the thousand and one questions which are addressed to him, and he must be prepared to act as guide, counsellor and friend to visitors from abroad and to those who use the telegraph only under the stress of domestic anxiety or grief. He has, in short, to be endowed with a big heart and much patience.

The instrument room, in which the telegram finds itself when it is shot from the tube, is well lighted and airy; and if the official ideal has been possible of achieve-ment it is square in shape. By means of moving-band conveyors the telegrams are kept constantly on the move from the time at which they are received in the office to the time at which they are disposed of and the "office drag", in other words the time spent on internal circula-tion, in the Central Telegraph Office, London, has been reduced by modern appliances from eight minutes to four minutes, which in the career of a telegram represents an important economy.

Considerable use is made of underground pneumatic tubes in London, Glasgow, Manchester, Liverpool and Birmingham for the conveyance of telegrams from out-lying post offices to a central transmitting office. There are 52 of these tubes between the Central Telegraph Office, London, and telegraph offices in the City and West End, the House of Commons, cable companies' offices and the offices of the principal newspapers and news agencies. Some of these are as much as two and a half miles long.

Errors in the transmission of telegrams are now, in these mechanical days of the teleprinter, very few and far between. During the era of Morse telegraphy, however, there were many amusing incidents due to errors for which inexperienced operators were responsible, although in fairness to the service it should be mentioned that such mistakes were usually detected and corrected by more expert telegraphists at a later stage of transmission. Due to the poorer quality of telegraph lines in those days, the dots and dashes of the Morse code were frequently either mutilated or distorted, and the received signals were not always clearly defined. But the change in only one or two letters sometimes produced astonishing results.

For instance, a message to an anxious and very new father informed him that a "deal box arrived safely both doing well." He probably had to think a little before he realised that he had become the father of a dear boy.

What appeared to be a somewhat belated news item reported that the body of a dead Roman (instead of woman) had been found in the Thames. There is no doubt that the recipient of a telegram of bereavement in which he was asked to "break the nuts gently" would have been much annoyed if the message had not been corrected before delivery.

A missing dot could cause a lot of trouble, and when such a small error in transmission could turn a chill into a child, the possibilities may be left to the imagination.

In those days, too, bad handwriting sometimes led to strange misreadings. A communication to "H.M.S. Oilcan" instead of "H.M.S. Vulcan" was fortunately corrected before it came to the captain's notice or there would probably have been an explosion on board. During a Cowes regatta week some years ago a report concerning activities on the royal yacht stated that "on the arrival of some distinguished guests the price of ales went up on deck". Of course it should have read "Prince of Wales", but maybe the press writer's thoughts were wandering. And the report of still another royal occasion recorded that "the band struck up the National Anthem as the King stepped on the jelly."

In another message a racehorse owner possibly anticipating success would yet have been surprised to hear that his horse had won by a week, instead of by a neck.

Abbreviations also had their dangers and were sometimes misunderstood. In the report of one political meeting it was mentioned that the candidate was received with "loud apples" instead of loud applause. And a collision in mid-channel between two "stmrs" was reported as having involved two *station-masters*!

These are only a few of the amusing slips of Morse days which tended to brighten the telegraph atmosphere. But the modern transmission of telegrams by telephone also causes some amusing howlers. The telegram addressed to a passenger on the "Cream Dairy", Southampton, on the occasion of a great liner's departure is a case in point. Another was recently addressed to the "1st Italian Grenadier Guards".

Arrived at the office of destination in the form of printed slip, which the deft fingers of the receiving clerk cut into suitable lengths and gum on to a delivery form, the telegram travels by pneumatic tube again to the delivery room where messengers are waiting under the watchful eye of an inspector. Over 1,300 boys are engaged on delivery work in London alone, as well as 100 motor cycles and 600 "push-bikes".

The many problems of manual—and pedal—delivery have been lightened by the increasing use of the telephone for delivery purposes. In London alone more than 4,500 telegrams are delivered daily by telephone to telephone subscribers, and in country districts the use of this facility of course saves an immense amount of work and time.

It is the aim of the administration to give the same quality of telegraph service throughout the country and pursuit of this object raises a set of problems in country districts differing largely from those in big cities.

There are now nearly 14,000 post offices in Great Britain and Northern Ireland at which telegrams are accepted from the public and the great majority of these are "scale payment" offices, where the sub-postmaster generally combines a Post Office agency with a private business. To these the substitution of telephone transmission for Morse was a great boon; often the old dot-and-dash procedure was terribly irksome. Delivery by telephone, too, helps the small sub-postmaster in a special way, for where this is not practicable he himself or probably some member of his family has to undertake hand delivery, often under most arduous conditions. The author recalls the pitiful wail of the sub-postmaster of a small village in the Cotswolds who, returning home on a Saturday evening in mid-winter from delivering one telegram, was faced by his reluctant wife with another which had been received during his absence. It entailed a three-mile walk through driving snow to a remote vicarage and the message, addressed to the vicar's wife, ran "Goodnight dearest, I am thinking of you, Daddy." The worthy parson had gone off to take Sunday duty elsewhere and the parting had evidently roused his most tender feelings. It aroused another set of feelings in the sub-postmaster's breast but the message was delivered.

That was a good many years ago and the vicarage is now no doubt on the telephone; at least one hopes so!

The habit of sending (as well as receiving) telegrams by telephone has grown very rapidly in recent years and is still increasing. Telephone subscribers are able to send and receive telegrams at any hour of the day or night; they are independent of their local telegraph office; if it is closed they are connected to the nearest open office. Moreover, telegrams passed in this way over telephone circuits are often expedited by escaping a handling at a branch or sub-office. Special facilities for handing in telegrams are not, however, confined to telephone subscribers; anybody may dictate a telegram from a public telephone call office, and the official who takes the call, with the assistance of the coin box, does the rest.

In order to prevent error through imperfect hearing, or more often through imperfect diction, the telephonist is required to repeat the message to the subscriber, spelling by analogy words and letters with similar sounds. This system, which is generally effective, has inspired a good deal of humour and it certainly tickles one's fancy to hear the word "post", for instance, described as "P for Peter O for Oliver S for Sugar T for Tommy". Why "sugar", one wonders, and not "Sarah" or "Sambo" since Christian names are generally used. There is probably a good answer somewhere.

There are various by-products of the telegraph system about which the ordinary man-in-the-street remains strangely ignorant. For instance there is the Night Telegraph Letter which provides a means of communication after the usual posting hour, and at a cheaper rate than by the ordinary telegraph service. The arrangement under which batches of one hundred or more identical telegrams are accepted for delivery at a very low rate recalls an outstanding occasion when 89,000 telegrams in one batch were handed in for transmission, addressed to possible subscribers to a new edition of the *Encyclopedia Britannica*, warning them that if they did not hurry they would be too late. The Post Office would probably like to see such publicity enterprise repeated; anyhow, the organisation is such that it would regard such an event with perfect equanimity. A visit to the Central Telegraph Office soon convinces one of this. Here more staff is employed than in any other telegraph office in the world. They handle about a quarter of the total inland telegram traffic, besides dealing with the bulk of the continental traffic and the radio telegraph traffic to ships at sea. Every day the "C.T.O." galleries deal with at least 150,000 telegraph transactions over more than 350 telegraph channels equipped at the London end with more than 400 tele-printers. At Christmas time the figure is doubled. The C.T.O. is open day and night, year-in and year-out.

The connection between the telegraph service and the Press is, of course, particularly close. Apart from normal services, for all great sporting events and other occasions of national and international interest a special telegraph equipment is rigged up on the spot and manned by the Post Office. International football matches, cup ties, test matches, race meetings—all have special local facilities for the acceptance and despatch of telegrams. When important assemblies meet, or important speeches are made by leading politicians, or others, the Post Office is always there to play its part in conveying copy to the distant printing machines. These "special events", as they are called in the telegraph department, of course necessitate a permanent and very flexible organisation to ensure adequacy and smooth running.

A short time back the Post Office set itself to dissect the telegraph traffic. Why in fact do people send telegrams? How far is the telegram a harbinger of bad news? Do financiers send longer telegrams than fishmongers? Are more telegrams sent on Wednesdays than on Thursdays? And so on.

To answer all these and a hundred other questions a careful analysis was made of all inland telegraph traffic for a complete week. 605,000 messages were dealt with. Two tabulating machines, designed for the last population census, ran day-in and day-out for nearly three months, by which time it was felt that all the useful information about the inland telegraph traffic was at last available.

Some very interesting facts came to light as the result of this census. First, it was established that 62 per cent of all telegrams are business messages and 38 per cent social in character. Of the business messages, the largest single category is formed by those sent by fish merchants, who account for 8·9 per cent of all telegrams. The fish, meat, fruit and kindred trades together account for about 12 per cent of the total traffic, and it is clear that the telegram plays a greater part in the buying and selling of perishable goods than in any other market.

On the social side the most interesting feature is the knock-out blow delivered by the census to the old idea that telegrams usually mean bad news. The Post Office has been trying to kill this "fear complex" for a long time but it dies hard. Indeed, we shall probably admit that many of us who are not habitual receivers of telegrams still accept the yellow envelope with a certain sinking feeling. However, as a matter of fact the census discloses that only 1·2 per cent of telegrams convey bad news, while 3·6 per cent carry congratulations of one kind or another. 5·8 per cent deal with betting, a steeply declining proportion, by the way.

The sending of congratulations is evidently inclined to make one a bit reckless, for telegrams of this sort are definitely longer than messages of other kinds, averaging

15·9 words each, while the average length of all messages is only 13·18 words.

Generally the census shows that, even under conditions of intense telephone development, there is a real use for the telegram as a written message meeting special needs in a unique way. By giving a clear picture of telegraph demand, the census will no doubt help the administration in adapting its rates and its services, its publicity and its methods, to meet the needs of the customer.

CHAPTER 8

FOREIGN TELEGRAPHS
AND WIRELESS

Telegrams can now be exchanged between every part of
the United Kingdom and almost every country or in-
habited island in the world, as well as some 15,000 ships
which are equipped for wireless communication.

Telegraph communication between Great Britain and
the Continent began in 1851 when the first Anglo-French
telegraph cable, containing four conductors, was laid
between the South Foreland and Sangatte. In 1853 a
cable containing six conductors was laid between Dover
and Ostend to provide an Anglo-Belgian service and
within the next eight years four more cables were laid
between England and the Continent.

The 1851 cable became known in Post Office service as
"St Margaret's—Sangatte No. 1". This cable was still in
use in 1937 after many repairs, but only one of its four
conductors was working and it has recently been decided
to abandon and remove it. In its early days it had a
curious adventure. It had been laid only a few months
when it was caught in a French fisherman's trawl, and
with a tenacity which in other circumstances would have
been praiseworthy it was brought to the surface. The
fisherman, realising no doubt that sea stories, and especially fishermen's stories, must be supported by tangible
evidence, hacked a length out of the cable and took it

*Deep sea cable: transfer from lighter to Post Office
cable ship*

home to Boulogne where he exhibited it as "a rare sea-weed with its centre filled with gold".

As long ago as in 1856 Cyrus W. Field, the American promoter of a project for a telegraph cable between the Old World and the New, first tried to awaken practical interest in it in this country. "The history of human invention", says Justin McCarthy, "has not a more inspiriting example of patience living down discouragement, and perseverance triumphing over defeat." Year after year abortive efforts were made; once, in 1858, the cable was actually laid and enthusiastic messages passed between Queen Victoria and the President of the United States. But after messages had been transmitted and received, more or less spasmodically, from August 10 to September 18, the effort, in the jargon of a more modern invention, "faded out".

Lots of people flatly refused to believe in 1858 that the miracle had in fact been accomplished, and one doubter in London was so vehement in his scepticism that he had to be taken in charge by the police. However, it was not difficult to establish the truth. A collision between two ships, "Arabia" and "Europa", off Newfoundland on August 15 in that year, was known in Liverpool two days later through a telegram signed "Cunard". Also, by two military messages sent from the Horse Guards to General Trollope, commanding in Nova Scotia, the return of the 39th and 62nd regiments to England was counter-manded and the British Government were thereby saved £50,000 in transportation charges. "Money talks" and this demonstration proved especially convincing.

In passing, it is pleasant to note that the record of messages which passed between Newfoundland and Valentia in this preliminary trial of the Atlantic cable does not once contain the signal "O.K." Yet we find from contemporary records of American telegraphs that this expression, which many of us have regarded as a modern invention, was in use by operators, and by the public as well, in the United States even earlier than 1858. Perhaps this evidence of a respectable antiquity will, for some people, soften the blow with which they hear it to-day, with other importations via Hollywood.

At last, in 1866, the first permanent cable was well and truly laid—2,000 miles of it—from Valentia to Newfoundland, along a seabed in some places more than two miles in depth. Success was achieved on a permanent basis and trans-Atlantic telegraphy had come to stay, to the discomfiture of some of the highest scientific authority in the land, which had repeatedly proclaimed it as utterly hopeless, wildly impracticable and indeed a sheer physical impossibility.

The continental telegraph service of to-day mainly radiates from the Central Telegraph Office in London. Most of the traffic passes over submarine cables, about 20 in number, laid between the south and east coasts of England to France, Belgium, Holland, Germany and Norway. These cables, generally speaking, are owned and maintained jointly by the Governments of the United Kingdom and the countries where they respectively land; the British share of maintenance is performed by His Majesty's Telegraph Ships—of which more later.

An interesting side-line in the functions of these cables is the Facsimile Telegraph service which is now worked between London and about 20 centres on the Continent. For the most part this service is used by the Press for the rapid transmission of news photographs, but drawings, plans and all varieties of printed and written matter can be transmitted in facsimile by this means. The examples of telegraphed photographs which we are growing accustomed to see in our daily newspapers indicate a rapid improvement in technical efficiency.

True to its reputation as a crime detector, the Post

Office will even undertake the transmission of finger-prints. Recently a Danish admirer of one of the B.B.C.'s successful dance bands desired to show her appreciation by presenting a bouquet to the conductor. She telegraphed her order to a London store and added a request that a picture of the gift be telegraphed back for her approval. The florist department of the store created the bouquet and the photography section took the necessary picture. This was rushed to the Central Telegraph Office and promptly transmitted to Copenhagen; in a short time the lady's approval was received. A considerable amount of facsimile telegraphy also takes place over the inland system. Transmission was practicable as far back as 1843, when a chemical process was invented, but it is only recently that the Post Office engineers have devised a really reliable and economic method. The invention of the thermionic valve, a very important milestone in the progress of electrical science, coupled with the use of the photo-electric cell, made it possible, without any pre-liminary chemical process, to transmit direct from the original object.

In addition to the cable circuits, the Post Office operates wireless telegraph circuits from London direct to several European countries. All the services are operated by the department's own wireless sending stations at Rugby and Leafield (Oxford) and its receiving station at St Albans. No messages are actually handled at these stations, which are in effect relay stations and are con-nected by direct lines with the message handling room —the Central Radio Office—in the Central Telegraph Office, London, where the actual messages from and to all parts of the country are concentrated. These direct wireless connections with European countries afford alternative routes to the cable telegraph circuits. They connect England with Czecho-Slovakia, Danzig Free Territory, Esthonia, Hungary, Italy, Latvia, Poland and

Rumania. Also, in the event of cable breakdowns due to storms or other causes, the Post Office can establish emergency wireless circuits with Iceland, Norway, Sweden, Germany, Holland and Belgium.

At one time the Post Office operated two trans-Atlantic telegraph cables, and also Beam wireless telegraph services with the Dominions, but in accordance with the recommendations of the Imperial Wireless and Cable Conference of 1928, these extra-European services were transferred to a British company which was formed for the purpose of co-ordinating the cable and wireless services connecting the various parts of the Empire. This company, which is now known as Cable and Wireless, Ltd., has a world-wide system and much of the extra-European traffic which is accepted at post offices, together with certain telegrams for Europe, is carried over the Post Office inland system to London or one of the other places where the company has an office. Here it is transferred to the company for onward transmission over their long-distance cable and wireless circuits. The control of the rates and services of Cable and Wireless, Ltd., is the concern of an advisory committee on which the Dominions and Colonies are represented.

Other companies also have cables landing in this country, and a message which the sender "routes" for these cables is accepted by the Post Office and transferred to the company concerned for transmission overseas. In many of the large towns these telegraph companies, like Cable and Wireless, Ltd., have their own offices. These are connected with the cable landing places and wireless stations by special wires leased from the Post Office.

Of the Rugby Radio Station and the rapid advances which have been made there in the application of wireless communication, the Post Office is particularly proud.

Wireless mast at the Post Office Overseas Radio-Telegraphy
and Radio-Telephony Station, Rugby

Rugby is one of the most powerful wireless stations in existence. It is in daily communication with almost every country in the world. Some people seem to think it has an even wider range than this. A number of messages have been received addressed to Mars and other long-distance destinations; they have no doubt been duly transmitted into space—for it seems a pity to reject good revenue—but so far no reply has been received, nor even a simple acknowledgment. The immense aerial system of the Rugby Station, occupying some 900 acres, can hardly escape the notice of passengers by the London, Midland and Scottish Railway. Its towering steel lattice masts, each five times as high as the Nelson Column in Trafalgar Square, which support the long-wave aerial system, are marvels of British engineering skill, and the unpretentious-looking building above which they soar contains the latest triumphs of the wireless engineer and the largest collection of wireless equipment assembled at any station in the world.

The masts are stayed with five sets of stays placed at intervals of 160 feet throughout their height; each mast is able to withstand a wind velocity of 140 miles per hour, as well as a horizontal pull of 10 tons at the top. The problem of complete insulation of the aerial wire was solved by pivoting the masts 17 feet from the ground on columns of insulators resting on granite blocks. The masts can be lifted slightly—with the aid of three 120-ton jacks—to permit the removal of cracked insulators. The earth system consists of buried copper wire following the plan of the aerial and extending 800 feet on either side.

The short-wave aerials are not nearly so spectacular as their taller neighbours. They are carried on self-supporting steel lattice towers, and each is constructed for transmission on a definite wave-length in a certain direction. Twenty-seven of these directional aerials—or arrays—have been erected.

Power supply is provided by the local electricity under-taking, and the bill presented to the Post Office each year shows a consumption of about 5 million units. By means of special generators high-tension direct current at 18,000 volts can be supplied to the plates of the valves of the long-wave transmitter. The primary control of the tremendous power radiated by the long-wave transmitter lies in the operation of a small and simple tuning fork. This generates, of course, only an infinitesimal part of the power ultimately used; actually this is amplified some 500 thousand million times by valves similar in principle to those contained in an ordinary wireless set.

Rugby Radio Station, in addition to its ordinary long-distance telegram and telephone facilities, broadcasts official press messages prepared by the Foreign Office for use free of charge in any part of the world. Certain copy-right news services are also despatched at fixed times for reception by subscribers on land and sea. The messages are actually transmitted from the Central Telegraph Office, London, which controls the Rugby transmitter by means of underground land lines. Rugby's part in the special service to ships at sea will be described presently.

The extent of the Post Office direct wireless and broad-cast services can be judged from the messages handled. On the direct wireless services, 600,000 telegrams (about 7,800,000 words) are dealt with on the average in a year, while the broadcast and press services average about 4,700,000 words.

The growing use of the ultra-short-wave system of radio telephony is an important feature in modern radio engineering. This wave has a limited range and is princi-pally used for transmission over short distances where the alternative would involve laying expensive submarine cables. Communication with Northern Ireland and with the Channel Islands is now partly covered by the ultra-short-wave system.

In the international telegraph system the tariff and rules are necessarily more complicated than in the inland service; one important feature is the downward graduation of rates for the benefit of messages which have no particular urgency—this has the effect of filling some of the spare capacity of the cable and wireless channels during the less busy hours.

The relatively high rates naturally charged on the long-distance service long ago stimulated inventive and economical minds to produce codes which compress into one chargeable word of five letters the meaning of perhaps a whole sentence. Code books have been developed to a very high pitch of ingenuity, and in the extra-European service over the busy routes as much as 90 per cent of the ordinary rate traffic is sent in code.

The general principles now current for the conduct of international telegraph, telephone and radio services were laid down by an International Telecommunication Convention drawn up at Madrid in 1932 and signed by nearly all the countries in the world.

The development of wireless telegraphy has been so spectacular since the War that one scarcely realises that its origin goes back into the last century. It was in 1896 that Marconi invented the first practical wireless system; it was immediately applied to the purpose of communication between land stations and ships at sea and between one ship and another. That, with all respect to the modern marvels of "broadcasting", still remains its most important service to mankind.

Before the days of wireless, when a ship was out of sight of land, she was as much cut off from communication with the rest of the world as if she had been on another planet, but to-day, thanks to the facilities offered by wireless, the crew and passengers of a ship, no matter in what part of the Seven Seas she may happen to be, can keep just as closely in touch with the world and its doings as if they were sitting at home.

There was a dramatic illustration, three years after the invention of wireless, of its usefulness for life-saving. In 1899, a year after the East Goodwin lightship had been equipped for wireless, she was rammed by a steamer, and the rescue of the crew was directly due to the wireless appeals for help. It was probably owing to this early demonstration of the potentialities of wireless signalling as a means of saving life at sea, that we were so well ahead of other countries in having our ships fitted with the necessary apparatus. But appreciation of the importance of wireless for safety purposes quickly spread and it is now compulsory in nearly all countries for ships above a certain tonnage.

The "ship-shore" service is not perhaps an unmixed blessing to the big business man seeking relaxation in an ocean cruise, or to the murderer escaping from justice. It was the Crippen case in 1910 which first demonstrated to the public at large the enormous possibilities of the new discovery. Dr Crippen, having murdered his wife, "Belle Elmore", fled to Canada in the S.S. "Montrose" with Ethel Le Neve who was disguised as a boy. Captain Kendall, the commander of the ship, noticed Le Neve squeezing her companion's hand. His suspicions aroused, he formed his conclusions as to the identity of the pair and despatched a long radio message reporting his discovery, as a result of which Inspector Dew, who was in charge of the case, sailed in a fast liner and was able to board the "Montrose" when she arrived at Quebec and make an arrest. Crippen, it is recorded, actually watched the transmission of the message reporting his presence on board, never dreaming how closely it affected him. "What a wonderful invention it is!" he remarked admiringly.

The service is operated by the Post Office. All round the country stations have been built so that, no matter off what part of the coast a ship may be, she is always within range of at least one station and thus in touch with shore. These stations are in three classes: the short-range coast stations; a long-range sending and long-range receiving station on the Bristol Channel; and the long-range sending station at Rugby already mentioned.

The short-range coast stations have a range of about 300 miles by day and considerably more by night. They are situated at Wick, the extreme north-east point of Scotland; Cullercoats at the mouth of the Tyne; Humber, near Mablethorpe on the coast of Lincolnshire; North Foreland at the mouth of the Thames; Niton, near St Catherine's Point, the southern extremity of the Isle of Wight; Land's End, the extreme south-west point of Great Britain; Seaforth at the mouth of the Mersey; and Portpatrick at the entrance of the Clyde estuary. Besides these stations in Great Britain there are two in Ireland— Malin Head, the extreme north point of the country and Valentia in the south-west; these are operated by the telegraph administration of Eire which is now of course entirely distinct from our own, but by an admirable working arrangement they are made to fit in with the general wireless organisation of the British Isles.

The telegraph communication service conducted by these stations shows a steady growth. It is found that 60 per cent of the total traffic is for business purposes, either concerning the ship itself or concerning passengers. The remaining 40 per cent consists of greetings or other social messages and arrangements for hotel accommodation on the ship's arrival.

An important feature of the work of the short-range coast stations is the control of messages when ships at sea are in distress. Throughout the whole of the twenty-four hours, at each of these stations, operators are listening for the S.O.S. signal which shows that a ship is in need of assistance. These calls are not frequent, but quite frequent enough; possibly one a week is a fair average throughout the year. When a S.O.S. is received, all other wireless working is shut down. The coast station asks the ship the nature of her trouble and whereabouts she is situated. This information is then passed on to the life-saving authorities and to any other ships which may be in the vicinity and all measures possible are taken to assist the ship and to rescue her crew.

The S.O.S. service with its dramatic appeal to the public imagination is, of course, well known. Equally familiar to the public ear is the broadcasting of navigational warnings. These are sent out by the B.B.C. on behalf of the Admiralty, to advise vessels of changes in navigation lights and buoyage, and of such perils as buoys breaking adrift, sunken wrecks, or floating wreckage. Listeners are also familiar with the warning notices issued by the Meteorological Office of the Air Ministry, containing information of approaching storms.

The short-range coast stations help the mariner in another way of which little is heard by the general public. There is a direction-finding service, by means of which an operator, on receiving a wireless request from a ship, can ascertain and communicate the direction in which that ship lies from his station, with an accuracy of within two degrees. Requests for this information are received on an average about 14 times a day. The usefulness of this service has led to the erection round the coast of 27 "Radio Beacons" which are operated not by the Post Office but by the various lighthouse authorities. They work automatically and send out at regular intervals of half an hour wireless signals from which ships fitted with the necessary receivers can pick up their bearings; in foggy weather the intervals are reduced from half an hour to six minutes.

The pair of long-range stations on the Bristol Channel, Burnham and Portishead, are provided with special apparatus which enables them to communicate with ships in any part of the world which are fitted with the corresponding apparatus. The two places form a single unit, the transmitting apparatus being situated at Portishead and the receiving apparatus 25 miles away at Burnham. Both are operated from Burnham, the link with the transmitting apparatus at Portishead being supplied by telegraph wires.

Of the telegrams passing between ship and shore, by far the heaviest load in this country is handled by the Burnham-Portishead unit. Short-wave communication, even between fixed points, is sufficiently complicated, but the successful handling of an enormous traffic load, when the distant stations are constantly on the move, presents a new set of problems. These, however, are being speedily solved. To the lay mind the ways of wireless are still very mysterious, and a mere expression of polite surprise was really inadequate to express one's feelings on being told by the officer in charge at Burnham that a case of "interference" recently experienced with short-wave reception there was traced to a police car signalling in the streets of Buenos Aires!

A "safety service" which deserves special mention is the medical service which is thus graphically described by Lt.-Colonel C. G. G. Crawley, R.M., M.I.E.E., the Post Office's Inspector of Wireless Telegraphy:

Many vessels when at sea, even though engaged on long voyages, do not carry doctors. Illnesses and ailments amongst the ship's company are generally dealt with by the captain so far as he is able to do so with the aid of the ship's medical chest. In serious cases, or where the captain feels that a doctor's opinion is desirable, he may forward particulars to a coast station in a telegram asking for advice. These telegrams are sent in plain language or in a special code which has been devised to meet the requirements of ships of several nationalities. By means of this code a telegram coded in one of these languages may be decoded into a correct translation in any of the other languages, and the difficulty which might otherwise arise with foreign ships is thus overcome.

Naturally messages of this type sometimes give rise to amusing incidents as, for instance, a report that a member of the crew had a pain in the port side of his stomach. In another case, where a patient had been stung by a tropical insect, alcoholic stimulant was recommended by the shore doctor, and a final report from the ship indicated that the patient was feeling much better and was thoroughly enjoying the treatment.

For ships which are not provided with the special apparatus needed to enable them to communicate with Burnham-Portishead, a special service is provided from Rugby. At certain times of the day this station broadcasts any messages which may have been received for these ships; the ships listen at these programme times and take down the messages addressed to them. This service is called the L.D.R. (Long Distance Radiotelegram) service. Although the ships to whom the messages are addressed are not able to reply, to ask for repetitions or even to acknowledge the receipt of the message, more than 99 per cent of the messages so sent reach their destination. In the course of a year some 90,000 words are transmitted by this service.

Rugby Station gives other services of great importance to ships at sea. In order that a navigator may find his longitude, it is of course necessary for him to know exact Greenwich time. For this purpose he carries one or more chronometers, but, however accurately a chronometer may be made, there will probably be some slight variation, which may have serious consequences. Nowadays, however, by means of wireless time signals the chronometers of ships can be checked at frequent intervals. Every day at 10 o'clock in the morning and 6 o'clock at night the standard clock at Greenwich Observatory is

connected by a telegraph wire to the transmitting apparatus at Rugby Wireless Station, and the time is broadcast.
These time signals can be heard all over the world, so
that wherever a mariner may be situated he is able twice
a day at least to find out the error of his chronometer and
so is helped to ascertain with complete accuracy the
position of his ship.

In order to ensure a constant standard of efficiency in
the wireless room on board British merchant ships, it is
laid down that operators must possess certificates of
efficiency issued, after examination, by the Post Office.
The examination is a searching one; the candidate must
not only demonstrate his ability to send and receive
wireless messages, but he also has to know thoroughly
the construction and maintenance of the apparatus with
which he will have to deal, and how to repair it if anything goes wrong. Nearly 1,400 candidates for the Postmaster-General's certificate are examined every year at
one or other of the 19 schools dotted about the country
where the would-be operators are trained.

The Post Office not only examines the operators; its
officials also periodically examine the ships' apparatus.
For this purpose there are seven inspection depots round
the coast, from which some 4,500 inspections are made
every year.

Until recently, all communications between ship and
shore had to be carried out by telegraph, messages being
transmitted by means of the Morse code of dots and
dashes. Consequently small ships, such as fishing
trawlers, which could not afford the luxury of a trained
wireless telegraph operator, were not able to take advantage of the communication facilities which the wireless organisation offered to larger vessels. The rapid
development of wireless telephony, however, has enabled
the facilities previously only available for large ships to be

extended to the smaller ones. At each of the short-range coast stations there is now installed transmitting and receiving apparatus for wireless telephony, and many small ships have been fitted with corresponding apparatus, so that now anyone on board is in a position to communicate with the shore and to send or receive messages.

This service is the subject of the film "North Sea", recently produced by the G.P.O. Film Unit. Here the adventures of an Aberdeen trawler in a violent storm are recorded, the principal actors being the trawler's crew and the staff of the Post Office radio station at Wick. This film, made by Cavalcanti and Harry Watt, has been hailed as the finest documentary film produced since "Night Mail".

Fishing vessels and other small craft can now be connected with friends on shore; one feature of "North Sea" is the conversation which the skipper has with his wife every evening at 8 o'clock. And passengers on the big liners can converse with subscribers in almost any part of the world.

It is no doubt vaguely realised that there is some connection between the Post Office and the B.B.C. but the strength of the link is not generally known. Some description of the Postmaster-General's functions in regard to broadcasting, apart from his privilege of answering questions about it in Parliament, may therefore be of interest, and will illustrate the responsibilities resting upon the Postmaster-General in regard to the control of wireless services generally.

First, a general allocation of bands of wavelengths to be used internationally for the various wireless services is made from time to time through the International Telecommunication Conventions, and it is the business of the Post Office, at the international conferences where these conventions are drawn up, to ensure that amid the pressing claims of other services such as air, ship, meteorological and police, the broadcasting service has an adequate share of available wavelengths. This share having been allotted on an international basis, it falls to the Post Office to see that broadcasting stations in this country get their fair proportion.

The next duty of the Post Office is to see that the programmes broadcast by the B.B.C. on the wavelengths thus secured are not interfered with by stations which, on one pretext or another, do not abide by their international agreements. Owing to the increasing number and power of stations, complaints of interference are more and more frequent and difficult to settle. The position is at present rendered particularly awkward by the rise in importance of the shorter wavelengths for long-distance broadcasting, and considerable difficulty is experienced in maintaining free from interference the short waves required for the Empire services.

The location, power and wavelength of each broadcasting station in this country are subject to the Postmaster-General's approval. Each broadcasting station is licensed after consultation with the Defence services; and it has to be ensured that the wavelengths used, the sites chosen and the masts erected will not cause interference or danger to those or any other public services.

The Post Office is responsible for the issue of licences for all wireless receiving stations, for seeing that these licences are renewed each year and for the subsequent accounting for the licence fee. The number of licensees is now well over 8,500,000. About 7,500,000 are in England and Wales, 800,000 in Scotland and over 100,000 in Northern Ireland. Some 47,000 licences are issued to blind persons, free of charge.

One of the most painful duties of the Post Office is to see that all receiving sets are licensed in accordance with law, and to trace the people who try to evade their responsibility. To trace unlicensed stations, a "comb" (or house-to-house enquiry) is made whenever there is reason to suspect unlicensed use of wireless apparatus in any particular district, and where evasion is suspected in the larger towns and areas special campaigns are undertaken, with vans fitted with wireless direction-finding apparatus. The Post Office is, of course, only anxious to see that listeners comply with the law, but it is reluctantly compelled to prosecute each year some 3,000 persons detected using unlicensed apparatus.

The Post Office also licenses and controls relay exchange systems which distribute broadcast programmes to subscribers by wire. There are about 330 relay systems, with some 250,000 subscribers. The Government recently reviewed the question of acquiring ownership of these systems but has deferred a decision until the end of 1939 when all licences will expire. Meanwhile, the possibility of the use of the telephone system and other means of distribution is being examined.

The development of broadcasting receiving apparatus and the extensive use of sensitive receivers have created many difficulties for Post Office engineers in the tracking down and elimination of causes of "interference".

The most common sources of this trouble, with which most listeners are to some extent familiar, are electric motors and generators, domestic appliances such as vacuum cleaners, refrigerators, hair-dryers and sewing machines, while trolley-buses and tramways, flashing signs and lifts are also very troublesome. In the majority of cases this interference is propagated along the electric light mains. It can usually be suppressed by the use of suitable filters, but special provision has to be made when some types of medical or X-ray apparatus are in use, as the patient acts as a miniature wireless transmitter and the whole of the outfit, including the patient, has to be surrounded by a metal screen.

There are 200 officers with 100 motor vans at present distributed throughout the country to deal with complaints of interference which number about 40,000 a year. The enquiry officer is armed with an ingenious "locator" which eventually leads him to the source of the trouble. When this is found a satisfactory filtering device is prescribed and the nuisance is overcome.

The Post Office has installed for the use of the B.B.C. a network of permanent circuits connecting the corporation's several stations. Some of these are specially designed for high-grade music transmission. Altogether these connecting circuits between the various studios and regional stations throughout Great Britain and Northern Ireland account for about 10,000 miles of wire.

In addition the corporation has power to requisition public trunk circuits as required for its outside broadcast activities, such as relays from theatres and running descriptions of special events. About 400 applications for these trunk lines are made to the Post Office every month; the lines connect the actual broadcasting point with the main network mentioned above.

In the international service, special circuits for the transmission of music have been constructed by the British Post Office and most of the continental administrations. The standard of quality of these circuits and the conditions under which they are made available for international broadcasts are laid down by the Comité Consultatif International Téléphonique on behalf of the telephone administrations, usually after consultation with the Union Internationale de Radiodiffusion, on which the B.B.C. and other broadcasting organisations are represented. Considerable use of the music circuits is made for the transmission of programmes, both from the Continent to the B.B.C. and from this country to broadcasting stations on the Continent.

The radiotelephone services operated by the Post Office are also used to a large extent for the transmission and reception of programmes between this country and countries overseas. On Coronation Day an "Empire Homage" programme of items originating in many parts of the Empire was transmitted over the Empire radio-telephone channels in such a manner that each of the countries concerned could receive and broadcast the whole programme; and on the same day the radiotele-phone services conveyed in addition 21 other items for broadcasting.

The ceremony in Westminster Abbey was transmitted over the Anglo-Continental telephone cables and broad-cast in twelve European countries. Descriptions of the procession in ten different languages were relayed to the Continent, necessitating the simultaneous use of six music circuits as well as a number of traffic circuits. Reports from abroad indicated that the ceremony and special commentaries were received most satisfactorily.

In the course of twelve recent months the Post Office provided facilities for nearly 900 broadcast transmissions to and from countries abroad; and it can readily be understood that the practical and successful accomplish-ment of so many transmissions from one part of the world to another for broadcasting is the outcome of exact planning and cordial co-operation with the British Broadcasting Corporation.

Great Britain was the first country to establish a public television service, and is still, in 1938, the only country in which television programmes can be regularly received in the home by the general public.

In May 1934 the Postmaster-General appointed a committee, under the chairmanship of Lord Selsdon, "to consider the development of Television and to advise on the relative merits of the several systems and on the conditions under which any public source of Television should be provided".

In accordance with the committee's recommendations, the B.B.C. was given the authority for operating the service and the London Television Station was opened in November 1936. The service is growing rapidly in popularity, largely because of its broadcasting of events of national interest ranging from the Coronation Procession to the Cup Final. A special cable between Broadcasting House and the West End of London enables pictures of ceremonies at such points as Whitehall and Hyde Park to be transmitted direct to the London Television station for radiation to viewers. For events farther afield a mobile transmitting unit is used which is connected by a wireless link with the Television Station.

CHAPTER 9

MORE ABOUT THE ENGINEERS

At the back of all the activities which have been described, ubiquitous but generally invisible, are the Post Office Engineers.

Some of their numerous activities have already been seen in the descriptions of the various services. We have caught, for instance, a glimpse of the part they have taken in connection with the transport of mails, in the simplification of the telegraph system, and more strikingly in the development of the telephone and in the application of radio to telecommunication services. Much, however, remains to be said about their work and particularly about their entity as a department of the great organisation which they serve in so many directions.

A glimpse of a bunch of wires in an open street-manhole, a long trench along the edge of a country road, vaguely attributed to some drainage development as we flash by, an occasional business-like dark green motor van with "Post Office Telephones" painted inconspicuously upon it and—a more intimate touch—the occasional visit of a mechanic to overhaul or improve our domestic telephone installation, these are the outward and visible signs of the Post Office Engineering Department.

This is, in fact, a very large and most important Post

Office department; its organisation, however invisible it may be to the naked eye, extends into every village, and its plant is in evidence along almost every road, railway and canal in the United Kingdom.

Put briefly, the function of the department is to provide and maintain the plant for public communication services, and to do so with the highest efficiency and at the lowest possible cost. It is in control of plant having a prime cost of more than £180 million; its expenditure on works and maintenance in 1937 was approximately £28 million, and the number of workmen employed is in the neighbourhood of 40,000.

The Engineer-in-Chief is responsible for the development, installation and maintenance of the electrical and mechanised plant and equipment required for all the Post Office services, including telegraphs and telephones, wireless stations, motor transport, submarine cables and all the various mechanical, lighting and heating installations.

The Engineering Department came into existence as a separate and distinct part of the communications system in 1870. In its early years it was mainly concerned with the provision and maintenance of the telegraph system. Gradually came the advance of the telephone and with that advance the Engineering Department, as we have seen, found its main activities diverted increasingly to the new service until the War brought progress to a dramatic halt, and turned the work of the Post Office engineers into channels of more immediate consequence.

It may well be imagined, then, that in 1919, when industry began swiftly to re-adjust itself and something like a boom began to appear, the Post Office found itself in a difficult situation. The problems which confronted its engineers were complicated by the coming of the automatic telephone, which has been described by scientists as the nearest approach of machinery to the human brain.

It was not exactly a new contrivance. It had been introduced into this country as far back as 1912 when the Post
Office inaugurated its first automatic public exchange at
Epsom, and by 1914 the system had been extended to five
other towns. At that stage, however, it was experimental
in character and it was only with the return to normal
conditions that the department was able to plan on a
large scale the conversion from manual to automatic
working of the telephone exchanges throughout the
country.

It aims to-day at a national telephone system which, in
quality of speech and speed of connection, will be independent of locality or of distance. Meanwhile technical
developments providing for the completion of trunk calls
on demand, reductions and modifications in tariff, as well
as the progressive conversion of manual exchanges to
automatic working, have popularised the service to an
extent which has at certain times during the past year or
two proved quite embarrassing. The difficulties of keeping
supply up to demand are being gradually overcome, but
not without causing a few grey hairs on departmental
heads.

The moment when the department is grappling with
these difficulties is, however, a particularly interesting
time to visit it and to see what the Engineer-in-Chief and
his staff are planning, not only to meet the situation
caused by a phenomenal growth of "telephone-minded-
ness" among the public, but also to provide for the future,
on the assumption that the growth will not only continue
but will gather increasing speed.

The engagement and training of additional men is, of
course, one of the most obvious ways to meet the situation, and indeed some 11,000 have been trained and added
to the strength within a couple of years. But an all-
important factor has been the excellent relations established and maintained with the manufacturers of plant.

Post Office lineman at work, Land's End

There are five key manufacturing firms for switching equipment and formerly all five, and the Post Office engineers as well, were experimenting and investigating independently. To-day they form a co-operative body, and the result is a pooling of ideas for British telephone development generally, and an allocation of each particular line of investigation to one individual member of the group.

A factor of outstanding importance in meeting the enormously increasing demand for long-distance telephone facilities has been the recent intensive development of the "carrier" system, under which a number of conversations can be conducted simultaneously over one pair of wires. During the last few years there have been great advances in this system, due to improvement in the design of amplifiers. Speech is a series of musical vibrations, and in telephone speech electrical vibrations are transmitted corresponding to the audible vibrations in ordinary speech. In carrier telephony these electrical vibrations are superposed upon a frequency which is greater than the ordinary speech vibrations. This same principle of the use of high frequencies for speech transmission is also the basis of radiotelephony and broadcasting. Indeed, the early carrier circuits on wires were obtained by adapting apparatus designed for radiotelephony.

In 1935 the Post Office decided to undertake a full-scale experiment with an installation giving as many as 12 simultaneous conversations on each pair of wires. Two special cables were installed for the purpose between Bristol and Plymouth and so successful has the experiment been that the 12-channel system, with repeaters spaced about 20 miles apart, will now be adopted extensively for the trunk traffic between the main telephone centres of the country. The continued expansion of long-distance telephoning will result, in a few years, in a complete network of carrier cables between all the principal towns. Cables laid during the last two or three years contain 24 pairs of wires affording a total of 288 circuits, in other words facilities for 288 simultaneous conversations.

But a much more significant development is at the present time taking shape. This is the co-axial system, under which the cable is replaced by a single copper wire surrounded by a flexible copper tube about half an inch in diameter. This tube is used to transmit a very wide range of electrical vibrations which includes the range of electrical waves used in radio broadcasting. A cable comprising four of these tubes has been laid from London to Birmingham with an extension to Manchester and is now being extended northwards through Leeds to Newcastle. As in the 12-channel system, speech in the two directions is carried separately, so two of the four tubes are required for telephony. They will provide no less than 400 circuits, which means that 400 simultaneous conversations will be carried. The remaining two tubes will be available for television purposes. The range of vibrations required for the transmission of television of the standard now being broadcast from Alexandra Palace is so great that one tube, capable of transmitting 400 conversations, is required for a single television transmission.

As an initial stage a group of 40 telephone circuits is working in the co-axial cable between London and Birmingham and the experience gained will enable the design of the equipment to be brought to a higher state of perfection. As time goes on and traffic expands, the demand for long-distance circuits will undoubtedly increase very rapidly; it is confidently hoped that the co-axial system will solve the problems which this demand will create. And it is a gratifying thought that the enormously increased circuit capacity of this new system is likely to lead eventually to a much lower cost.

It has already been shown that the policy of the Post Office, in the development of all its services, is to give the small rural community facilities which will bear comparison with those of its big neighbours. The problem of carrying out this policy in the telephone service has presented many difficulties.

In what may now be called "the old days", since progress in telephony has made such rapid strides in twenty years, these rural areas were served, so far as they were served at all, by exchanges operated manually and available only during the day. Since the number of calls was small it was not economic to have a full-time operator. Consequently a local store, perhaps, was utilised, where the storekeeper took on the telephone just as one item in a large stock of goods which it was his business to serve out to customers. Or the telephone would be added to the responsibilities of the local sub-postmaster.

As soon as automatic systems had been introduced in the larger communities, the engineers turned their attention towards making rural exchanges automatic, and as such they now exist in considerable numbers. Subscribers have the advantage of a service at any hour of the day or night, and a service, moreover, free from the hazards of a human operator who might be subject to the occasional distractions of retail trade. The Post Office on the other hand benefits not only by the sale value of an improved service, but also by avoiding the search for the suitable part-time operator. And instead of being bound to the premises to which the operator is attached, it can place its exchange at the most convenient and central point in the area to be served, in a small, self-contained, untenanted, simply-constructed building accessible only to the engineers.

The plant for these exchanges is built on the unit principle; one unit consists of the equipment necessary for serving 25 subscribers and the smaller exchanges consist of eight units. Thus each of these exchanges has a capacity of 200 subscribers. In addition to being able to dial anyone else on the same exchange, the subscriber can gain access to the outer world by dialling a special code which connects him automatically with the most convenient manual exchange.

Recently the unit system has been extended to the smaller urban communities. On these new and improved exchanges 800 subscribers can be accommodated. Each subscriber is able to obtain for himself a subscriber on any exchange within about 15 miles. The fee may vary from 1d. to 4d. according to distance; the equipment determines the correct charge and registers it on the calling subscriber's meter for accounting purposes. The caller is also able to reach more distant exchanges by dialling a certain code which will give him access to an operator on a "parent" exchange. These parent exchanges are suitably named for they will watch the unit exchange with a motherly eye; and in this they will have an advantage over human parents—the faults of the children will be registered and brought to notice automatically.

In the present circumstances anything that puts the brake on development is rather deplorable and in this connection the worst enemies of the Post Office engineers are storms. Once or twice during the past few years the race to supply telephone service against popular demand has been seriously impeded by damage due to violent weather conditions. There are generally two or three bad storms in the course of the year, and the methods of dealing with the damage caused to wires and equipment have been thoroughly organised so as to restore the service to normal conditions as quickly as possible.

The damage of course occurs mainly to the overhead system. Underground the cables lie more snugly and the Engineer-in-Chief plans every year to increase their mileage. Only about 15 per cent of the long-distance channels now remain in the open. But there is necessarily a vast mileage of local and junction lines, and a good deal of damage can be done to these by a howling gale or a blizzard.

The Engineering Department's records of a severe storm which began in Northern Ireland late in the evening of January 19, 1936, may be quoted as an illustration both of damage done and of the steps taken to repair it. A very heavy fall of snow was followed by a westerly gale which reached a velocity of over 90 miles an hour. 6,000 poles were put out of action; 2,000 were laid flat and the rest were either broken or tilted over into all sorts of queer angles. The wires had become heavily coated with snow and ice and thousands of miles of them were brought down.

At that time there were only two long main underground cables in Northern Ireland (it will comfort telephone users in that area to know that the position has since been immensely improved) and consequently practically the whole of the service in an area of 5,000 square miles was disorganised. All exchanges were cut off from Belfast, and most of them were also cut off from each other. In addition to these trunk and junction lines, some 6,000 subscribers' lines (about one-fifth of the whole) were put out of action. There were certain exchanges where every subscriber's circuit and every junction line had been severed, the operators being left with absolutely nothing to do. The ultra-short-wave radio link for trunk services between Northern Ireland and Great Britain obtains its power from an overhead power line and this was also brought down by the force of the gale acting on the heavily ice-coated surface. It was indeed a storm of a very special kind! And to make the problem of the Post Office more difficult there was a shortage of stores owing partly to storm damage in other parts of the United Kingdom, but more particularly to heavy demands for cable and other material required for the provision of special circuits during the last illness of King George V.

The first step was to establish contact with out-station inspectors and linemen and get them to prepare rough preliminary surveys of the damage in their area. Since the ordinary means of communications were not available, the military authorities were asked to help and messages were soon passing over the army wireless system. The ordinary Works Control now became "Storm Control". As reports came in, motor transport and gangs of men were allocated to various sections of the country. Controlling officers met every morning in Belfast to determine the quickest methods of restoring the services and to draw up plans of action. Everyone worked with determination. Some 300 miles of single-pair cables were run out along hedges, walls and fences to bridge the gaps, and by this temporary expedient partial service was restored to all the larger towns in two days. In another two days only 23 small outlying exchanges remained isolated from Belfast; these were in the more mountainous and inaccessible parts of the country where the snow still lay too thick to permit the transport of men and stores; it took still a further two days before service could be restored to these points.

While the repairs to trunk and junction routes were being carried out the 6,000 subscribers' lines which had been broken down were being attended to, and by the night of January 21 most of these had been restored. So that in two days from the first fury of the storm the service was working again. The main repairs would, of course, take months to complete, deflecting a material amount of energy from the work of construction, but temporary and effective service was being rendered by means of engineering feats which seemed at the time little short of miraculous.

Apart from its vast network of land lines the Post Office through its Engineer-in-Chief controls and maintains some 5,000 nautical miles of submarine cable containing 25,000 miles of conductors connecting the inland system of communications with that of other countries and also with islands off our own coasts; estuaries are crossed by the same means. For the maintenance of these cables the Postmaster-General has two cable ships officially styled "His Majesty's Telegraph Ships", the *Monarch* and the *Alert*, each with a displacement of about 1,000 tons. They operate from depots at Woolwich and Dover and each carries a crew of about 65 officers and men. The *Monarch* is proud successor to the original ship of the same name launched in 1883. The old *Monarch* laid the first telephone submarine cable in the Channel and was engaged in active Post Office service until her loss in 1915. On September 8 of that year she was proceeding down-Channel in hazy weather to effect repairs to a damaged cable when she struck a mine off Folkestone and sank within three minutes. Three men lost their lives and a number were injured. But for the excellent discipline of the men and the resourcefulness of the officers the casualty list would have been much bigger. Some of the survivors escaped by the boats, many were picked up from the sea. The new *Monarch*, to quote Captain F. G. Ramsay, the Submarine Superintendent, is "a beautiful ship in every way, a magnificent sea boat and a real little lady".

The two cable ships may only lay two or three new cables a year, but they carry out between them about 100 repairs of varying importance and difficulty. One commission may entail a complete circuit of the British Isles and may last three months or more. The Post Office cable ships fly their own flag, the Blue Ensign with the badge of the department in the "fly"—Father Time seated on a coil of rope, looking with apparent indifference at the hour-glass in his right hand being shattered by a flash of lightning, symbolic of the annihilation of time by the electric telegraph.

The work of the cable ships is hazardous and difficult in calm weather, but even in the face of storms and fog the task of maintaining the lines of communication goes on. Many relics of wars and past storms have been brought to the surface during repair operations. On one occasion an old anchor was raised to the surface near the Goodwin Sands and its peculiar characteristics identified it almost certainly as a relic of the Spanish Armada; unfortunately this relic disappeared mysteriously during the War.

Among the Engineer-in-Chief's many responsibilities is the maintenance of the Post Office motor fleet of over 16,000 vehicles. This fleet covers in the aggregate about 160 million miles a year and consumes about 9 million gallons of petrol. For control purposes the country is divided into 10 motor transport areas, each a self-contained unit, with an area officer and staff responsible for all forms of motor transport within the area, whether used for postal, engineering or stores purposes, and whether used in big towns or remote villages.

Large users of motor transport usually concentrate their repair work. The Post Office follows a different plan. It maintains about 20 repair centres in each area. These centres vary considerably in size; some, in the big cities, look after as many as 300 vehicles; others, in country districts, may have no more than a score in their charge. In all they provide full time employment for 1,000 mechanics. These men are recruited outside the service but the drivers of the vehicles are all found from within. In the postal service the duty of driver and postman is combined, and there are now 11,000 of these postmen-drivers.

In the engineering service, too, the driver combines driving with his normal duties as an engineering workman.

One of the most vital functions of this department is research. In the improvement and elaboration of communication services it is not content with the discoveries of outside scientists and foreign administrations. At Dollis Hill, in the north-west of London, it has its own research station and here Post Office engineers live constantly and excitingly on the very edge of knowledge.

The Engineer-in-Chief and his research officers must keep in touch with all phases of science, some of which may have no apparent connection with Post Office problems at all. The latest discoveries and inventions must be studied carefully to see if there is any possibility of using them for the improvement of existing services or the development of new ones. And all the time there has to be a close watch on the commercial and financial effect of applying any particular discovery to Post Office use. Research is going on all over the world; the results must all be gathered and absorbed at the Dollis Hill laboratories.

One of the most interesting studies at present being pursued there is that of the possibilities of the photo-electric cell, which varies an electric current when its illumination is varied. One outcome is a device which is being developed for the mechanical "facing-up" of letters, with their stamps all in the correct position for cancelling.

The full possibilities of the photo-electric cell are by no means yet fully realised; they are working on it day and night at Dollis Hill. One of its most popular accomplishments is the Speaking Clock, familiarly known to Londoners as "TIM". The origin of "TIM" as one of the new telephone services has already been described, but enquiries as to "How it works" are so numerous that a short technical description may not be out of place.

The announcements of time are made verbally from records, and each announcement is followed by three "pips" or "tones", the last of which indicates the announced time accurately to one tenth of a second. The clock consists of a motor-driven shaft on which are mounted four glass discs, like gramophone records, which are made to revolve at a constant speed. The announcements are recorded photographically on the glass discs and the reproduction of sound is accomplished by projecting a beam of light through the discs on to a photo-electric cell. Thus, as the discs revolve, the intensity of light falling on the photo-electric cell is varied and this, in turn, causes variation in the electrical characteristic of the cell. By the use of associated electrical apparatus the variations of electrical energy are converted into sound at the telephone receiver. The changing from one announcement to another is effected by moving the optical system so that the light is projected through a different part of the disc. The clock is checked by an hourly signal from the Greenwich Observatory and a reserve clock can be switched into service immediately if the regular clock fails.

"TIM" was brought into use on July 24, 1936, and from that date the number of calls to the clock has steadily increased until it now averages well over 300,000 a week. This represents revenue to the telephone service at a rate sufficient to pay for half the upkeep of the research station. Ample switching equipment has been provided to give simultaneous announcements of time to a large number of callers, but to defeat any tendency on the part of a fascinated caller to listen to the Golden Voice indefinitely a device has been introduced which cuts it off after about a minute.

In the Dollis Hill laboratories it is possible to see under test mechanisms connected with every side of the Engineering Department's activities, from extremely

Post Office London Railway

complicated valve-operated switches which will enable a London telephone operator to call a subscriber in, say, Birmingham without the co-operation of her Birmingham colleague, to a lacquer which the research chemists have applied over the gum on stamps. The lacquer comes off pleasantly when licked and does not prevent the stamp sticking to the envelope, but it does prevent several stamps sticking together while in the automatic stamp selling machines.

Another machine, recently constructed at Dollis Hill and first used at Folkestone, announces verbally when a desired number is "engaged", replacing the tone signals which sometimes cause confusion to subscribers. Research into the problems of acoustics bears valuable fruit in improving the performance of telephone instruments. The interests of those who find the use of the telephone normally difficult are not forgotten; telephones have been designed for subscribers with very weak voices and for those who are partially deaf.

Increase in the length of telephone circuits brings numerous interesting problems for solution such as that of "echo", which manifests itself in the subscriber hearing the echo of his own voice reflected from the far end of the line. Much original work in connection with this problem has been done at Dollis Hill and has led to the production of simple and highly efficient voice-operated devices, which overcome the trouble by clearing an electrical path ahead of the speaker's voice while blocking the return path to his ear.

The research station includes a training school equipped with apparatus which represents the very last word in the science of communications. There is accommodation here at one time for about 600 students, who are drawn from all parts of the country. Training is confined to the automatic telephone and other complicated systems which necessitate costly demonstration equipment. There are six subsidiary schools about the country for the training of the staff in duties requiring sound craftsmanship but rather less intricate equipment.

This scheme of training in departmental schools supplements the technical education which the workmen obtain from technical schools and colleges in various parts of the country, and supplies that up-to-date and exact knowledge of the handling of complicated apparatus which the technical schools are unable to provide.

CHAPTER 10

THE POST OFFICE AS BANKER AND STOCKBROKER

There are still people of whom one hears occasionally who regard an old stocking, or the cavity under the loose board, as the best repository for spare cash, but the spread of education and the growth of the Post Office Savings Bank side by side must surely have brought the number of such hoarders down to something quite small. At all events the Post Office Savings Bank has given us some figures which demonstrate not only the good sense and thrift of the nation as a whole, but also—if demonstration were needed on such a point—the increasing faith and growing interest in a stable system of government and a settled order of things in general. For the bank has to-day 10 million customers, or nearly one in four of the whole population of Great Britain and Northern Ireland, and new accounts are opened at the rate of about a million every year.

It was Daniel Defoe, imbued no doubt with the methodical habits of Robinson Crusoe, who first conceived the idea of a savings bank. This was in 1689 and at least his fundamental idea of entrusting the savings to the Government, in consideration of the payment of interest, survives. Over a century passed before Samuel Whitbread, in 1807, revived the idea, and was able to submit his plans to Parliament. He was the first to propose entrusting the management of the banks to the Post Office, but his scheme was not accepted.

The honourable title of the "Father of Savings Banks" is usually given to the Reverend Henry Duncan, of Ruthwell, Dumfries-shire, whom one might call the Witherings of the Post Office Savings Bank. In order to encourage thrift among his poor parishioners, Mr Duncan founded in 1810 at Ruthwell a small bank which was the forerunner of a great new national movement. The savings which he collected were not entrusted to the Government but were placed on deposit with one of the commercial banks, at that time paying 5 or 6 per cent interest. The interest received, after deductions to cover the cost of management, was shared among the depositors. Control was in the hands of a court of directors consisting of local people of influence who gave their services voluntarily.

Strict enquiry was made into the family affairs and moral character of the proposed depositor, fines were imposed if a minimum amount of 4s. annually was not deposited, and the rate of interest could be varied at the discretion of the directors in accordance with circumstances. Thus, for example, a depositor who intended to get married received 5 per cent, while his more cautious fellow who remained single got only 4 per cent. Such penal measures and encouragements to matrimony formed no part of the administration of the Edinburgh Savings Bank, which followed in 1814. Here all depositors received the same rate of interest. No moral test was applied to qualify them as depositors; they were simply given a deposit book and they could deposit and withdraw as they pleased.

To say that the immediate success of this institution was the basis of the Scotsman's reputation for extreme thrift may not be historically accurate, but it is a fact that in two years there were 70 banks established in England on similar lines. The Government of the day were not slow to see the importance of the new movement, and, anxious to encourage it, they passed an Act offering to the new banks the privilege of investing their surplus funds with the National Debt Commissioners at the rate of 3*d*. per cent per day or £4. 11*s*. 3*d*. per cent per annum. Encouraged by this measure of State security, more than 500 banks were established in the United Kingdom within the next year, each bank being controlled by trustees and managers.

The experience of the succeeding years showed the possibilities of development, and in 1859, following a Government inquiry into the subject, Mr (afterwards Sir Charles) Sikes of Huddersfield proposed a scheme, a feature of which was that every money order post office should have a savings department. In this same year Disraeli, in an ill-fated Reform Bill, proposed that a vote should be given to persons who had £60 in a savings bank. This clause provoked much ridicule. Suppose, it was asked, a man with £60 saved drew out a few pounds to get married or save an aged parent from starvation. Why should he be disfranchised as a penalty for such very human action? This, however, is a digression into politics. The Bill, anyhow, was thrown out as being a little too clever and the Government went with it.

The Sikes scheme was, however, developed by Mr Chetwynd, an officer of the Money Order Department (who became first Controller of the new bank), and was accepted by Gladstone—then Chancellor of the Exchequer—as the basis for his Post Office Savings Bank Bill, which became law on May 17, 1861. On September 16 of the same year the Post Office Savings Bank came into being. Lord Morley tells us that Gladstone, reflecting in later life on his legislative work, placed the

Post Office Savings Bank Act among the three finest achievements of his career.

On the opening day 435 deposits amounting to £911 were received; incidentally the first five deposit books were issued to the five sons of Mr Chetwynd, the bank's first Controller. The idea caught on so rapidly that by the end of the year 1,676 post offices were open for Savings Bank business. Early in the next year the system was extended to Scotland and Ireland, and by the end of the year 1864 no less than 3,081 offices were established throughout the United Kingdom, which of course in those days included what is now the Irish Free State. By 1870 the number exceeded 4,000 and the deposits in that year amounted to £6 million, the total amount due to depositors on December 31 being £15 million. To cut short a long story of successful growth, the corresponding figure for 1880 was £33 million; for 1890, £67 million; for 1900, it was £135 million; for 1910, £169 million; for 1920, £267 million; and for 1930, £290 million.

Early in 1938 the amount standing to the credit of depositors approached £500 million. In the previous year a record jump of £42 million had been made.

To-day Post Office Savings Bank business is transacted throughout the United Kingdom at over 17,500 post offices, open every week-day in every town and nearly every village, and no matter where the depositor may have opened his account, he can avail himself of the bank's many services at any of them.

The popularity which the bank has always enjoyed must be mainly attributed to the advantages secured under the Act of 1861: the absolute security offered—the repayment of deposits with accrued interest is backed by all the resources of the State; the fixed interest—the rate of $2\frac{1}{2}$ per cent has never been varied; the ubiquity of the service—the account holder is not restricted to the office at which his account was opened, but can make deposits and withdrawals at any Savings Bank post office in the land; the acceptance of the smallest savings for any individual depositor—even for a child under seven; the provision for corporate savings; and also the guarantee of secrecy.

Attempts have been made to arrive at a detailed classification of the people to whom the bank appeals but it is difficult to do so. The simple form which the depositor is asked to sign on opening an account provides for "occupation"; but the information supplied is frequently vague, and many female depositors describe themselves merely as married women, widows or spinsters.

A recent test, confined to newly opened accounts, gave the following results (married women and widows are left out of account because of the uncertainty as to occupation):

	Males (per cent)	Females (per cent)
Wage-earning classes	60	49
Salaried classes	20	17
Scholars, students, children under 7	11	14
Independent (including those who gave no occupation)	9	20

Recent years have been notable for the steady growth of co-operation between the three national thrift agencies —the Post Office Savings Bank, Trustee Savings Banks, and the National Savings Committee (with its Scottish counterpart the Scottish Savings Committee)—in the advancement of the National Savings Movement, of which His Majesty the King is patron. The special services which each of these organisations can offer have come to be recognised as complementary to the services of the others, and together they provide a comprehensive national savings system which the small saver may use according to his individual needs, in the full knowledge that his money is absolutely safe.

The National Savings Committee was formed in 1916 for the purpose of promoting the sales of National Savings Certificates. It has its headquarters in London, and a Regional Commissioner and staff in each of the 12 regions in England and Wales, to assist the work of its army of voluntary workers numbering over 100,000. Upwards of 37,000 National Savings Groups of various kinds are at work under its auspices, of which some 23,000 are in schools. In recent years the provision of facilities for the weekly collection of sums for deposit in the Post Office and Trustee Savings Banks has been added to the functions of National Savings Groups. Of the total number of these groups at work, 83 per cent provide combined facilities for deposit in a Savings Bank and investment in National Savings Certificates. The Scottish Savings Committee works on similar lines in Scotland where there are about 1,400 Savings Groups.

Sir Max Pemberton, writing in commemoration of the bank's 75th anniversary, said something which will be appreciated not least by his fellow-survivors of a derided century:

Booksellers tell us that this is an age of history and biography rather than of fiction. Many capable writers misuse their leisure in abusing Victorianism. Stern-visaged people point out the enormities of an age which lacked the cinema, knew nothing of mechanised music and was nevertheless supremely self-satisfied. Rarely do we hear anything of achievement in the Nineteenth Century. Yet, surely, when the ultimate story comes to be told, two phases of Victorianism will be remembered with gratitude and wonder. The Education Acts of the 'sixties, how fitting that they should march step by step with the Post Office Savings Bank Act of 1861! As the nation began to read, so it appears, it began to save on a national scale. Learning to write, it could append a signature to the page of a bank book where formerly a "mark" had served. By reading, it verified its bank balance and was content. Arithmetic permitted it to add up the sum of its savings, and so, in later years, to bow to the genius of a mechanical audit. Thenceforth, the movements marched *pari passu* upon a mission which has made this country the richest in the world and able to-day to declare her finance paramount—at once her pride and her security.

Let us now take a more intimate look at this institution and its internal economy. The Headquarters Building of the Post Office Savings Bank stands on a site which was once an annexe to Olympia and the scene of thrilling and spectacular rescues of the Deadwood Coach by Buffalo Bill and his gallant cowboys from the attacks of blood-thirsty redskins. In any one of the five main workrooms a hundred yards race could be run, and altogether some 350,000 square feet of floor space are provided. The bank was removed to its present position in 1903 from Queen Victoria Street, where it occupied the site of what is now Faraday Building. When the bank outgrew its quarters it was decided to make a really good job of the removal, and since there was no particular benefit to be gained by keeping it in the City it was taken to a hitherto unheard-of address—Blythe Road, West Kensington— an address which has probably since appeared at the head of posted communications many times more than any other address in the world.

Since the removal practically the whole of the vast site has been built upon to cope with increased business and to-day the authorities are once again beginning to feel the need for more room. Decentralisation of work in the case of this department of the Post Office could only be wasteful and confusing, and so Headquarters has to deal with 140,000 transactions every day, involving over £740,000, while its yearly outward correspondence exceeds 700,000 items, excluding bank books returned after audit. A staff of 4,000 is employed, of whom 2,900 are women.

The inward letters are often quaintly humorous, sometimes consciously so, as in the case of the fond parent who wrote, "I have not filled in my daughter's occupation, which is at present 'cutting teeth'." But the unconscious specimens are the best.

Every depositor who so desires can nominate someone to receive his deposits at his death, which explains this one: "Kindly send me another nomination form", wrote a widow. "My husband has passed away and I wish for another."

"I beg to notify you of the death of Mrs —— and amongst her defects a Savings Book has been found."

The Lost Book Branch has many a knot to unravel. "Will you kindly send me on a new book as I had a fire and want to put some money into it."

"After another look round I have found the book down at the back of my secretary" (many old "secretaires" contain traps of this kind).

The marriage of a woman depositor of course involves changing her name in the department's records and in her deposit book. This sometimes causes trouble.

"I regret that I cannot forward a marriage certificate," wrote one new bride, "but I have a dog licence which is in my married name."

"I wish to inform you that I was married on September 26 according to the rules in the deposit book."

And on the other hand, the plaintive reply to a routine question asked in a case of doubt, "No, I am not married. Please put it right."

Sometimes the seamier side of marriage is disclosed. "I cannot send my book as requested, as my wife has used it to singe a fowl." And again, "The £8. 10s. which is in my husband's bank book is money I have

Port of London: the river postman

given him out of his wages to put in the bank for our holidays."

Then the coming of a family brings its own set of comedies. A young mother wrote: "I am thinking of putting my baby in the Post Office Savings Bank. I know we are unable to draw him out until he is seven years old."

Facilities for the young are one of the features of the administration and many accounts are opened on the day a child is born, the deposits made from time to time being repayable, as the last-quoted mother was well aware, at any time after the child is seven. Indeed, small savers in every sense of the term have always been well catered for. In 1880 a slip with spaces for twelve penny stamps was introduced, to help those who found it difficult to keep their pennies until a shilling accumulated, the slip being accepted for deposit in a Post Office Savings Bank account when twelve stamps had been affixed. Originally introduced experimentally in certain counties in September 1880, the scheme proved in a few months so successful that it was extended to the rest of the country. It brought the benefits of saving within the reach of the poorest. To these a shilling was perhaps a large sum, but many were able to save penny by penny. Within six months 576,000 completed slips were received and they led to the opening of more than 220,000 new accounts. The appeal of this idea of "looking after the pence" was specially strong to children, who opened 250,000 accounts in the course of the next three years.

Among other bright ideas for helping the small saver was the introduction of "Home Safes" in 1911. The home safe is an ideal means of saving unconsidered trifles and hence its popularity survives, in spite of the following caustic criticism of a certain newspaper when it first appeared:

Talk of grandmotherly legislation! The Post Office now proposes to issue pretty little money-boxes to the public and keep the keys. The idea is that you put pennies in when you are in a penurious mood, and then you can't touch them, however thirsty you may be, without making a preliminary pilgrimage to the nearest Post Office. We suggest that our Sunday bib and tucker should be kept at Scotland Yard, lest it be soiled on week-days.

About 400,000 home safes are sold every year at 1s. each, so "grandmotherly legislation" evidently still has its appeal. The contents of a home safe may be used either for deposit in a Post Office Savings Bank account or for the purchase of Savings Certificates.

At the luncheon which the Lord Mayor of London gave in honour of the bank's 75th anniversary in 1936, a silver home safe was presented by Major Tryon, the Postmaster-General, to the Duke of Kent for the use of Prince Edward. Contrary to all precedent the key was presented with it; as a rule the key is kept by the Post Office.

A guest at this luncheon was Mr G. H. Dunn, a watchmaker of Fenchurch Street, the hero of a very human little story. Mr Dunn saw a reference in his newspaper to the pending anniversary and wrote to the Director:

I have had an account in the Post Office Savings Bank, as far as I remember from what my father told me, since 1862, so as I have been a depositor continually since that date I reckon I am one of the oldest of the depositors. My father on the first birthday of each of us (his family of four) opened the accounts. We each had a money box, started when we were born, into which we used to put 6d. a week, and on our birthdays it was deposited in the Bank and given to us when we were 21 years, to put our own savings in also. I should like to know if this is so, if not giving you too much trouble. Yours obediently, G. H. Dunn.

A typical example of family thrift which received an answer equally typical of the spirit of friendliness and unstarchiness, if one may coin a word, which pervades the Post Office of to-day:

Dear Sir, I am very glad to have your interesting letter of the 11th instant. Your account was opened for you by your mother, Mrs Elizabeth Dunn, on the 31st March 1862 and, so far as is known, no other of the ten million accounts with which the Bank deals goes back as far. I feel sure that an announcement that so fine a record may be claimed by a Londoner will be of interest to the guests at the Guildhall luncheon. May I add that the Bank is very proud to have served you for more than seventy-four years and hopes it may continue that service for many years to come. Yours faithfully, E. B. Steers, Asst. Controller.

And following the letter came an invitation from the Lord Mayor to the Guildhall luncheon.

It may be mentioned in passing that the Savings Bank has turned out at least two famous men in its time though their fame lay in different directions. One was W. W. Jacobs. He served in the department from 1883 till 1899. It was in 1896 that he leapt into fame with *Many Cargoes*, to be followed swiftly by *The Skipper's Wooing* and *Sea Urchins*. At that stage it had become evident that his vocation lay more in the direction of making people laugh than in looking after their savings, so he gave himself up entirely to writing.

The other was Michael Collins, the Sinn Fein leader, who was ambushed and shot in Ireland in 1922. He was a boy clerk at the bank from 1906 till 1910, living during that period with a sister in West Kensington. He left to go into a stockbroker's office in the City.

The "Society" section of the bank is worthy of special mention. Here are handled the accounts opened by all sorts of clubs and societies for banking the funds contributed by their members. There are 45,000 of these accounts and the diversity of purpose of the various organisations is particularly interesting. There are Botany, and Blanket, Christmas Tree, Coal, Pig and Cycling Clubs. Soup Kitchens, Bands of Hope, Women's Institutes, Parish Magazines, Musical Societies, Flower Shows, Temperance Societies and Masonic and other Lodges are represented. Scouts, Guides and Churches entrust their funds and there are even (an appropriate end to the list) Hearse Funds. Almost any corporate organisation can open an account provided it is not trading for profit. Navy and army personnel can make full use of the bank whether serving at home or abroad. There are special arrangements to meet the men's convenience.

The evolution of banking practice, so far at least as the Post Office is concerned, has followed lines which are very familiar in the procedure of such institutions: first a nervous stringency of regulation, inclined to make things rather difficult for the client, followed gradually by a genial relaxation, and in later years by a veritable fever of concession and a flood of facilities designed to meet every reasonable need of the depositor and to make banking as attractive and simple as may be.

The first need of the great majority of depositors is to know that they can get their money out with a minimum of delay. There is always the pressing case like that of the depositor who wrote on his withdrawal form, "I require the money urgently as I am always falling into areas with my landlord." So the process of withdrawal has been made progressively easier. Sums up to £3 can now be withdrawn on demand at any Post Office where Savings Bank business is transacted; up to £10 can be withdrawn by telegraph in a few hours; and the normal process of withdrawal by notice and warrant sent by post is now operated so that the money required can usually be made available at any named post office two days after the posting of the notice; larger sums require three days' notice. A depositor requiring still speedier service can ask in his notice of withdrawal for the authority to be telegraphed, and thus get his money the next day.

Formerly there were limits to the annual deposits and the total amount which could be held by an individual depositor. These limits were abolished during the War and now any sum, up to £500 in a calendar year, may be deposited. Cheques are accepted, also dividend warrants, postal orders and money orders.

Two fairly recently introduced facilities show the keenness of the Post Office to meet its customers' convenience in this as in every other department of its activities. First the "Travel Warrant". These warrants, which are supplied in small booklets, are of the fixed amount of £3 or £5 each, and may be cashed at any Savings Bank post office without the surrender of the bank book. A depositor can obtain any number of warrants up to six at a time, subject always to his having a sufficient balance in his account. This facility is specially useful to depositors on holiday.

The other, also specially designed for holiday-makers, is the "Cruising Credit", which enables a depositor going on a cruise on a British ship to have any sum from his account placed to his credit on board. A credit certificate is issued to the depositor, who can withdraw the whole or part of his credit upon producing the certificate to the purser. Any balance remaining at the end of the cruise is returned by the shipping company to be credited to the depositor's account. It cannot be said that the Post Office, in catering for the modern holiday spirit, has failed to move with the times. And this obliging banker will now, on receipt of instructions, make periodical payments without further trouble to the depositor in respect of insurance premiums or house purchase instalments, and will even pay his telephone bill! The main requirement on the part of the depositor is to keep an adequate balance in his account; overdrafts are strictly taboo—it is the only inhuman feature in an otherwise human and considerate organisation.

Lord Bridgeman's Committee on the Post Office credited the bank with "a high degree of enterprise" and added, "We do not think it is going too far to say that the Savings Bank is ahead of any comparable private concern in the adoption and development of office mechanisation and labour-saving devices." This process began in 1926 when the application of machinery to the posting and balancing of depositors' accounts began. This involved a change over from ledgers to a system of cards. A machine types on the card the entry of the deposit or the withdrawal as the case may be, and at the same time casts the entries for purposes of the daily balance. Started experimentally on a small block of accounts, mechanisation proved successful and was gradually extended to the remainder. The whole process of converting over 10 million accounts took three years. As a result of the reform economies amounting to nearly £150,000 a year have been achieved, operations have been speeded up, and numerous improvements have been effected in service to customers. This pioneer effort was keenly watched by many of the big joint-stock banks, and the example of the Post Office Savings Bank has been widely followed.

In addition to this office machinery the bank has its own printing plant and envelope-making machines; and practically all the books, forms and envelopes required for its vast business are produced on the premises.

The funds of the Post Office Savings Bank are controlled and invested by the National Debt Commissioners. They have a Post Office Savings Bank Fund to which is credited money received on deposits, less payments in respect of withdrawals. A monthly statement of the balance due to depositors is published in the *London Gazette*, and returns are presented to Parliament annually showing the amount of the liabilities to depositors, details of the securities held against these liabilities, the income, expenditure and the resulting profit. Of this, 5 per cent is retained in the fund and invested in a provision against the depreciation of securities and the residue is paid to the Exchequer, or in other words goes back to the depositor in his corporate capacity as the British Taxpayer.

At the beginning of the Great War the Savings Bank afforded striking evidence, first of the initial shock to the nerves of the public, and then of the rapid restoration of confidence. During the week in which war was declared 200,000 notices of withdrawals were received for £3,200,000 as compared with 80,000 notices for £650,000 in the corresponding week of 1913—scarcely a "run on the bank" but at any rate a mild manifestation of uneasiness. But within a few days warrants for £500,000 were returned to be cancelled and in many instances when warrants were cashed the money was redeposited before it left the Post Office. By the third week of war, withdrawals were below normal, and in the last quarter of 1914 deposits exceeded withdrawals by over £500,000.

After the War it was wisely decided by the Government that the gratuities payable on demobilisation should take the form of credits in the Post Office Savings Bank. Thus 3,500,000 accounts were opened with £56,000,000 to their credit, an immense task which was done under great pressure because simultaneously there was rather naturally an almost overwhelming flood of withdrawal notices. However, a substantial residue of the money "stuck", to form a nest-egg for many an appreciative ex-service man in the lean years that came later.

The Postmaster-General, in addition to his other excellent qualities, is the cheapest stockbroker in the land. It was in 1880 that depositors in the Savings Bank were first enabled to purchase Government stock through the bank's agency. There had been some agitation for this facility for many years but, with a nervousness characteristic of the times, the idea was repeatedly rejected, because it was felt that the Savings Bank Fund would be weakened by the withdrawal of money for investment, and that trouble would arise with investors through fluctuation in price and depreciation in capital values. The first objection has been proved to be unsound; but the downward trend of prices in the early years of the century showed that there was a good deal of force in the second.

The opposition to this scheme prevailed for some time but it was lessened by the argument that there were less than a quarter of a million people with an interest in British funds, while in France the holders of *rentes* numbered more than 4 millions. After a stormy passage a Bill was enacted and it became possible to hold, through the medium of the Savings Bank, stock to the value of £300, the number of stocks open for investment being limited to three. In six weeks there were 2,230 investments representing £130,000 of stock. When war broke out there were 180,000 holders of stock amounting to £26,500,000.

In 1915 the Chancellor of the Exchequer decided to use the Savings Bank for the purpose of attracting small subscriptions from the general public for the 4½ per cent War Loan. Over a million holdings were added to the register during the six weeks' subscription period. The policy of opening the Post Office register to the general public, and not only to Savings Bank depositors, has been followed in the case of all succeeding issues of stock. In 1920 there were 4,600,000 holdings in the Post Office register representing £224,500,000 stock and bonds. This was the high watermark so far as the bank is concerned.

We have seen how the small investor, "discovered" as long ago as 1880, was encouraged and multiplied during the war years for the purpose of the War Loans. A further invention mothered by the necessities of war was that of Savings Certificates. These were first issued in 1916 on the recommendation of a committee appointed by the Chancellor of the Exchequer under the chairmanship of the Rt. Hon. E. S. Montagu, M.P. At the time expectations about this new device as a money-getter did not run high, but a veritable passion for thrift was discovered as an underlying trait of the British character; the most sanguine hopes of the optimistic minority in financial circles were vastly exceeded and, up to the present time, the number of certificates issued is not less than 1,300 millions.

The terms of issue of Savings Certificates have, of course, been revised from time to time since the War to conform with the fluctuating rates of interest at which the State has been able to borrow; there have in fact been six issues, beside a special conversion issue for holders of the first issue, but the changes have not in any way affected the certificates previously issued.

A unit certificate of the current issue costs 15s. and becomes worth 20s. in ten years. The 5s. increment is spread over the whole period in a manner cunningly designed to discourage any desire to "cash in" until the end of the period. Thus at the end of the first year 3d. interest is added; during the second year ½d. is added at the end of every completed period of two months; thereafter ½d. is added at the end of each completed period of one month up to the end of the tenth year. A bonus of 3d. is added at the end of the fifth year, and a further bonus of 3d. at the end of the tenth year. This represents a rate of interest of £2. 18s. 4d. per cent per annum over the whole period of ten years.

National Savings Certificates are primarily intended as a long-term thrift investment for individuals and cannot be held by registered companies, public bodies or firms. And in view of the advantageous terms offered, which include freedom from income tax, no one person may hold more than 500 units. But the certificates may be bought by any person in the name of another, by two or more persons in their joint names for their joint benefit, or by one or more persons "in trust for" another.

It is not difficult to understand the popularity of this particular form of thrift. The ordinary small man who wants to invest and save is a little bewildered by the jargon of the Stock Exchange, the brokerage charges, the fluctuation of values, and so on. In Savings Certificates he has a simple form of investment that can be purchased with a minimum of formality at a post office or a bank, very handy in form, redeemable at short notice practically anywhere in the United Kingdom, and having behind it the security of the State. The capital value of the certificates is not subject to market fluctuations, but it increases steadily at a rate which if not spectacular is at least attractive, as things go; moreover, the purchaser knows about it at the time of purchase and can rely on it. Thus a purchaser can budget definitely for the future in the knowledge that his forethought will not be upset by some wayward trick of Fortune. And, as a crowning benefit, the interest earned is not subject to income tax!

There is a special use of Savings Certificates which ought to be mentioned. Employers of labour are making increasing use of endowment and group life insurance schemes, based upon the investment in National Savings Certificates of contributions made by employers and employees. Conditions are flexible and can be fixed to meet an individual firm's requirements. Amounts contributed by the firm in this form of provident scheme are an agreed trade expense for income tax purposes, and the limit of a holding of 500 units does not apply.

And, lastly, in the administration of the money invested there is an important provision under which local authorities may borrow up to 50 per cent of the amount spent in the purchase of National Savings Certificates in their respective areas; so that half the money goes back to the service of the town or county where it was earned— a far-seeing and statesmanlike contrivance.

The task of dealing with National Savings Certificates falls to the Money Order Department of the Post Office. This department is also, as its name implies, concerned with the remittance of sums of money through the post by means of money orders, postal orders and trade charge orders. Further, it deals with the payment of old age and widows' and orphans' pensions throughout the United Kingdom. The progress and distinction which glorified the early years of Queen Victoria's reign are surely reflected in the number of centenaries which we are at present celebrating, or thinking of celebrating. Among the first of these is the centenary of the Money Order Department. It started in a very small way but to-day its offices in Manor Gardens, Holloway, house some 3,000 employees.

The original money order was a contrivance of six officials known as "Clerks of the Roads" to check the theft of letters containing coin; these thefts were very frequent at the end of the eighteenth century in spite of the fact that detection involved execution. The Post-master-General agreed to bear the cost of advertising this plan, and allowed the advices of the "Money Letters" to pass free under the frank of the Secretary of the Post Office. The profit, if any, went to the Clerks of the Roads.

The limit of the amount which could be transmitted by this means was five guineas and the commission, of which the payee paid half, was sixpence in the pound. In addition there was stamp duty to be paid and also double postage, since each article sent by post had to be paid for, and the Money Letters had naturally to be enclosed in an ordinary letter. This latter imposition was for a time evaded by printing the money order at the head of a large sheet of paper, of which the lower part could be used for correspondence. There is on record the case of a very trustful remitter who escaped all the expenses of a money order by consigning to the post a £5 note simply folded and bearing on the back of it the address of the consignee.

The Money Letter plan proved a success and on December 6, 1838, money order business was taken over by the Postmaster-General. The rates of commission were then fixed at 6d. for amounts not exceeding £2, and 1s. 6d. for amounts not exceeding £5. The maximum limit was raised to £10 in 1862 and to the present limit of £40 in 1904. In consequence of reduction of the commission brought about in 1871 the number of orders issued reached the total of 18 millions, the highest number ever attained. The low rates for the small orders led, however, to a loss in operation and this situation was met by the introduction, in 1881, of the postal order, by which money could be remitted more simply and cheaply, and with no loss through heavy overhead charges.

The money order has now to compete in the lower ranges of value with the postal order, and up to £40 with the growing use of the cheque. British banks have in recent years much extended their facilities for keeping small accounts. The Money Order Department has kept abreast of this development and has arranged for the payment of crossed money orders through the banks. At the present time about 60 per cent of inland money orders are not paid at post offices at all, but are handed to banks for collection either at the General Post Office in

London, or locally. Such clearances in bulk relieve the Post Office of much counter work, and there is no question of the advantage of the crossing arrangement to the public.

Inland money order traffic grew from some half million orders in 1840 to fourteen and a half millions in 1920 (representing £102 million). Since then the increasing popularity of the postal order and the introduction of the Cash on Delivery service for inland parcels have contributed to a reduction in traffic until it is now only about half what it was at its maximum.

The genesis of the Overseas Money Order service is especially interesting. In 1843 Sir Rowland Hill foreshadowed the exchange of money orders between the Mother Country and her Colonies, and the subject was re-opened six years later by the Directors of the New Zealand Company. It was not, however, until the Crimean War broke out and the special need of the troops for some means of remitting money home was demonstrated that the Overseas Money Order service began. During 1855 Florence Nightingale remitted for the troops as much as £50 in a week, and at the end of that year it was decided that the Army Post Office should issue money orders at inland rates at Constantinople, Scutari Headquarters and Balaclava.

In 1859 a reciprocal exchange with Canada was arranged and thereafter the system was rapidly extended to other colonies. In 1868 the first convention with a foreign power was concluded, Switzerland being the pioneer country. Belgium followed suit in 1869, and other countries in quick succession.

The Great War brought its special problems of fluctuating exchange rates, and, of course, in some cases the service had to be discontinued. In more recent years, with the depression in international trade and widespread currency difficulties and exchange restrictions, Overseas Money Order business has fallen away materially, but there are welcome signs of a revival here, as in industry and trade in general.

The postal order—which has been aptly called "the poor man's cheque"—was introduced in 1881 to deal simply and speedily with the lower grades of money transmission. At first only a few values were put on sale, but now the number of different denominations has been greatly expanded to meet public demand. At the outbreak of war in 1914 the Government withdrew gold from circulation and postal orders were elevated temporarily, by Royal Proclamation, to the status of currency, being issued, of course, free of poundage for that purpose. In a few months, however, when treasury notes became available, postal orders resumed their normal function.

In the last ten years sales of postal orders have much more than doubled. The number sold annually is now about 350 millions. One of the chief causes of the phenomenal growth of the past three years especially has been the increasing popularity of football pools. Of all the characteristics of the great British public one of the most profitable from the point of view of the Post Office is that unquenchable faith that one fine day a sixpenny postal order and a happy guess will bring a fortune. Post Office counters in many towns are thronged towards the end of the week by pool fans waiting their turn to buy low value orders. At the Money Order Department itself a single consignment of as many as 60 mail bags, containing about 1,500,000 postal orders, is a commonplace sight during the football season.

The vast quantities of paid postal orders which arrive every working day in the postal order branch of the Money Order Department for audit are examined and checked against the claims made by postmasters and banks who paid them. Many types of labour-saving machines are in use as in other large accounting establishments, but there is one type of machine in the Money Order Department which is peculiar to the Post Office. This is the Macadie-Ratcliffe Sorting Machine which sorts the orders into values and into numerical sequence and treats about 11,000 orders per hour. It is believed to be the only machine made that can handle such flimsy documents. The Post Office takes legitimate pride in this ingenious invention, because it was designed by Messrs Macadie and Ratcliffe of the Post Office and constructed in one of the Post Office factories. Fifteen of these sorting machines are installed and each is worked to capacity.

The total volume of the remittance services which the Post Office performs to-day can only be conveyed by a further use of "astronomic" figures. Altogether the number of remittances dealt with in a year is 366 millions, or say 35 for every family in the United Kingdom, and the amount remitted is about £177 million or roughly £17 per family.

CHAPTER 11

STORES AND SUPPLIES

The magnitude of the Post Office services will suggest the existence of an extensive organisation for the supply of material to enable these services to carry on. Actually the Stores Department of the Post Office, with its factories and depots, employs a staff of over 4,500 and occupies in the aggregate an area of about 35 acres. It is responsible for the material requirements of the daily working of the entire Post Office machine. It keeps the postman supplied with uniform; it sees that new and growing communities have their pillar boxes, stamp-selling machines and telephone kiosks; it stocks the 24,500 post offices throughout the country with stamps and postal orders and all other requisites for the transaction of business; it furnishes "big business" (through the Engineering Department) with its private telephones and telephone exchanges and teleprinters and equips the individual telephone subscriber with his instrument and directory; it supplies the postal service with mailbags, string, labels, seals and motor vans, and the engineers with their tools, poles, wires, cables, batteries, apparatus and all the essentials of the telegraph and telephone service. It provides all the multitudinous forms and pads, tickets and books, and general accessories for the whole of the staff scattered over the country from the Headquarters establishments to the small village sub-offices. The 150,000 uniform-wearing servants of the Post Office regard the Controller of Stores as their tailor, hatter and outfitter. They look to him even for the annual issue of the medal ribbon to which they may be entitled by military service.

Altogether it is a very extensive and complicated business which is administered from the headquarters of the department in Bedford Street, Strand. And it is astonishing to find how much the activities of this department are affected by each change or development of Post Office policy. To take a simple illustration—the reduction two or three years ago in parcel postage rates, accompanied by an increase in the upward limits of weight, would at first sight seem to call for no more than a variation in the rates of printing of the different values of postage stamps. As a matter of fact, among many other tasks which had to be completed in the two months which elapsed between the announcement of the changes and the date they came into operation, the department had to provide additional weights to 24,000 post offices, replace 12,000 spring balances carried by rural postmen, and arrange for the alterations to the dials of the weighing machines on 1,100 post office counters. Also in many cases motor cycles and side cars had to be substituted for push cycles, and small motor vans had to be replaced by larger vehicles. It is on occasions like this that the manufacturers of Post Office supplies show the stuff they are made of, and this time His Majesty's Prisons also showed their mettle by a big increase in the output of mail bags.

The department maintains two factories, one in London and one in Birmingham, for the repair of telephone and telegraph instruments, and for the assembly and manufacture of special equipment. Each employs about 850 people; the majority of the men are known as telephone mechanics, a class which is peculiar to the Post Office factories. In addition there are cabinet makers, french polishers, instrument makers, fitters, tool makers, carpenters and blacksmiths. In order to maintain a trained staff, there are generally about 120 boys assisting in the lighter work, and acquiring the rudiments of their craft. The staff at each factory includes about 170 women and girls who are engaged chiefly in such work as coil winding, engraving, metal polishing, french polishing, and switch-board cable forming.

Practically all the work of the factories is done on a piecework basis, which allows the average worker a fair profit; in addition an examination premium is paid on all jobs which pass an electrical test without undue rejections. In all cases, of course, the time rate of the worker is guaranteed, and the time rates of all the trades-people correspond with those paid in outside industry.

While some manufacture is carried on, the bulk of the work other than repair is that of the assembly of apparatus to meet special requirements; this, from its special and non-recurring nature, is not suitable for mass production by the trade.

The factories have assembled a great many hand-microphone telephone sets in standard colours, and have produced all the instruments demanded to date in special shades of colour to fit in with individual colour schemes. The patterns sent by customers for guidance range from pieces of wood to strips of dress material and scraps of feather; no one from north of the Tweed has yet thought of ordering a tartan telephone!

One of the many miscellaneous services rendered by the factories is the taking of about 1,200 X-ray photographs every year for the Post Office Medical Department. The operator is a mechanic who in his private capacity is a serving brother of the Order of St John of Jerusalem.

The main function of the factories is, however, the repair and reconditioning of apparatus returned to store. A steady stream of such apparatus flows into the depots adjacent to the factories, where it is graded after joint inspection by a factory foreman and an inspector of the Engineering Department. These two officers decide whether an item is worth repair; if it is not, it receives a dab of blue paint, and is conveyed to the scrap heap. Articles in need of major repair receive a dab of red paint; those in need of minor repair, a dab of green; while those needing only a rub with a polishing rag, or slight adjustment, are appropriately given a touch of white.

All items repaired have to pass the same examination as new stores, and must be in fact "as good as new". Indeed, after examination and test, all the apparatus, new and repaired, is stocked together without distinction. The cost of repairing and bringing the apparatus up-to-date, taking everything into account, from the actual cost of the necessary raw material or parts, up to the due proportion of the pay and pension of the Controller, averages about one-third of the cost of the article if supplied new from the contractor. The annual output of reconditioned stores from both factories at corresponding new value is about £1,250,000.

At ten ports round the coast there are depots for the treatment and storage of telephone poles. Normally the Post Office buys about 120,000 poles every year; between 50 and 60 sizes of poles are regularly stocked, covering a wide range in size from a "light" pole of 16 feet in height to a "stout" pole of 85 feet. As many poles as possible, some 15,000 a year, are obtained from home forests, principally the New Forest and the Scottish Highlands, but about 87 per cent come from abroad, particularly from Norway, Sweden and Finland. The bark is removed before the poles are examined by the department's inspectors. As soon as possible after they arrive at one of the ten pole depots, they are dressed, generally by machine, to make them shapely, and undergo the necessary cutting and boring. The poles are then stacked for some months until they are seasoned sufficiently to receive the treatment required to make them durable. This involves a process of impregnation with creosote under pressure up to 150 lb. per square inch. All this processing is carried out by contractors under the supervision of the department's inspectors, who meet the ships on arrival and watch the poles through all stages .of preparation.

Stores for the postal as distinct from the engineering service: uniform and protective clothing, mailbags, printed matter, stationery, scales, date-stamps, publicity matter, string, seals, etc., are held mainly at Mount Pleasant, Clerkenwell. This depot is on the site of the old Clerkenwell Prison. All traces of the prison building have now disappeared, but for many years the uniform clothing section was domiciled in the old prison chapel and bakery, with several rows of eligible cells thrown in for storage.

To meet the needs of its army of uniform wearers, the Post Office buys every year about 280 miles of cloth, 500 miles of cotton fabrics, 1 million yards of tape and braid and over 4 million buttons. The supply of uniform clothing is an interesting branch of the work of the Stores Department. It is not a simple matter of ordering a suit of clothes made from a roll of cloth selected by the customer. The Post Office tailoring contractor supplies only one item, the thread for sewing the garments. All the rest—the cloths, linings, tapes, braids, buttons, buckles—are purchased separately from the manufacturers. Texture of material and correct shade and fastness of the dye are important matters of detail. The inspection of the lining, materials and all other items including the finished garment is performed by the department's staff at Mount Pleasant, and for this purpose a chamber having controlled conditions of temperature and humidity is maintained there. Bales of cloth are compressed under hydraulic power in order to reduce the storage space required.

The measurements of each uniform-wearing officer are recorded in the Stores Department and these records form the basis of the periodical manufacturing demands which are placed with tailoring contractors. In most cases the measurements coincide with those of one of the standard "fitting sizes". A well-known tailor placarded London with a picture of a very prosperous looking individual of enormous proportions who was being measured by a poor insignificant-looking tailor with two measures tied together. The legend under the picture was: "We take extreme measures to satisfy our customers." The Post Office could make this boast with some measure of truth. There are 450 sizes for postmen's tunics, each with four lengths of sleeve, but even the generous provision of these 1,800 fittings leaves a number of outsize men whose garments have to be specially made for them.

However, in spite of the varying physique of the personnel, misfits are only about 2 per cent and these are largely due to increasing bulk or possibly the results of "slimming", not reported to the Stores Department.

Standards have improved considerably since Mr Pickwick's day. Mr Jingle, it will be remembered, when surveying himself in the glass after borrowing Mr Winkle's suit, remarked: "Rather short in the waist, ain't it? Like a General Postman's coat—queer coats those—made by contract—no measuring. Mysterious dispensations of Providence—all the short men get long coats—all the long men short ones."

King George's Coronation was made the occasion for the issue of a smarter and lighter uniform specially for summer wear. For a long time, postmen had been clothed throughout the year in 22½-ounce all-wool serge, which in summer time must have been somewhat trying. The new material is three ounces a yard lighter.

The evolution of Post Office uniform is an interesting subject. It was Aberdeen, strange to relate, which first went to the expense of ordering its post into livery—it was to be of blue cloth with the arms of the town worked in silver on the right sleeve; this was in 1590. Two hundred years later red was chosen for postmen's uniform to signify the development of the service from the royal couriers who conveyed the King's despatches. The scarlet piping on the modern uniform is the sole relic of this splendour. For some time only the upper part of the body was treated to uniform; the men were required to provide their own trousers, and one of the arguments put before the Treasury by the Postmaster-General of the day, Lord Walsingham, in seeking authority to spend £500 on these uniforms, was that they would make it easy to observe letter carriers if they frequented ale-houses or pawnbrokers' shops when they ought to be delivering letters! Not unnaturally the letter carriers resisted the change as a reflection on their honesty, and moreover objected that a distinctive dress would single them out as persons probably in possession of large sums of money.

Needless to say the humorists seized on the absence of trousers from the official issue and *Punch*, which still, by the way, has its Post Office joke practically every week, took exception to the scarlet coat as elevating the postman into a formidable rival to the policeman in affairs of the heart. It was not till 1860 that trousers were added to the official equipment. By that time the initial uniform bill of £500 had grown to £18,000; to-day, though the splendour of bygone days has given place to a smart simplicity, the annual bill is roughly £250,000.

For the manufacture and repair of mailbags, the Stores

Department purchases and supplies to His Majesty's Prisons about 1,250,000 yards of canvas every year. There is a story, by the way, that a prison visitor came across a late eminent financier engaged on this work of national importance in Maidstone Gaol. "What you! Sewing!" he exclaimed. "No!" was the reply, "Reaping!"

Distribution of postal stores generally follows a more or less regular routine. There is a general issue of uniform to the uniform-wearing staff twice a year, winter and summer, and the postmasters replenish their stocks of stationery once a quarter and of stamps and postal orders weekly, fortnightly or monthly according to the size of the office. It is possible to group the destinations in such a manner that the stores flow in and out of the main postal depot evenly throughout the year and provision is made well in advance for the peak load of demands which always comes at Christmas.

Distribution of engineering stores proceeds along quite different lines. Each work requires its own parcel or consignment of stores, be it the hundreds of poles and miles of wire required for erecting a telephone trunk line, or the individual telephone instrument for a new subscriber. A gale of wind, especially if it be accompanied by a fall of snow, may increase the normal daily demand tenfold. Every week the store depots meet approximately 14,000 requisitions from engineers and 15,000 from postmasters. Each week they receive about 1,500 tons of new stores and material as well as a heavy tonnage of recovered stores returned for reconditioning or scrapping.

For the distribution of new stores and collection of old the department employs a fleet of 66 motor vans, lorries and cars ranging in size from an eight-wheeled float with hoisting gear, designed for the transport of drums of lead-covered cables, down to the speedy one-ton town-delivery van. All towns within a radius of a day's run from the store depots may have a regular weekly delivery of stores. For the more distant towns and the more occasional runs the department relies largely upon hired transport. The annual mileage covered approximates to 750,000, and 25 per cent of the total weight of stores dealt with is transported by this means. The remainder is sent by passenger or goods train, by canal barge, by sea, or by post.

The disposal of obsolete store and scrap material is a profitable side line in the department's business. Condemned apparatus, lead-covered cable and gutta-percha-covered wire have a negligible sale value in their original condition and they are accordingly broken up into their component materials. Nearly one thousand ounces of platinum and precious metals are removed in the course of a year from instruments of which they form the electrical contacts. The baser metals, like brass, nickel, iron, aluminium, nickel silver, are accumulated in separate lots. Lead-covered cable is cut up and fed to melting pots in order to separate the lead and copper; no fuel is purchased for the furnaces, the heat being provided by waste wood from other condemned articles. Gutta-percha is stripped from its copper wire and macerated for further use in the manufacture of carriers for the pneumatic tubes serving the telegraph offices. There is no waste that careful study can obviate.

A considerable proportion of the scrap lead is sold to contractors for making into lead seals for mailbags, but the more general means adopted for disposing of scrap material is sale by tender. The lots are keenly sought by the trade and the proceeds from a year's sales may reach £200,000. The principal items are 2,500 tons of copper, 2,000 tons of lead, 300 tons of string and 200 tons of canvas.

The Stores Department has special responsibilities in regard to stamps. Much interest has been shown in recent stamp issues, not only by philatelists but by the public generally. We seem to be becoming more and more concerned with the beauty—or at least the effect upon the eye—of articles in common use, and recent postage-stamp developments have well merited this interest.

The Edward VIII stamp was a definite break from traditional design; it represented the first use of a photographic portrait in place of the traditional engraving from an artist's drawing. Moreover, it seemed to meet the modern taste in the lack of decorative design. It was in fact revolutionary, and the confidence with which it was issued was tinged with some slight anxiety. How would the public take it? It turned out to be most popular. There was a certain amount of criticism but this came chiefly, and naturally, from artists, who, however revolutionary they may be in their own sphere, mostly draw the line at photographs!

The King George VI stamps are a compromise between the ultra-modern Edward VIII and the traditional George V issue. There is a return to the artist's conception of the King's head and to a certain amount of decorative elaboration, though this is kept within pleasing limits. This issue, too, has been very popular and leaves no room for doubt that the Postmaster-Generalship of Major G. C. Tryon will remain memorable in philatelic history. It was due to his personal initiative and encouragement that the commemorative coronation stamp was issued in face of great difficulties and in the shortest time on record. Some 500 millions were printed and disposed of during the two months for which this special stamp was on sale.

The production of stamps is from first to last an interesting process. The initial selection of a design is by no means as simple a matter as it sounds. Many suggestions are made and many studies submitted, the treatment of the King's head and the selection of the surrounding decorative detail cause much anxious thought. Advice is sought from the Royal Fine Art Commission and the Council for Art and Industry. Then one day the *Court Circular* announces that the Postmaster-General has been received in audience by the King. His Majesty has approved a design and the actual work of production may be put in hand.

Every year about 7,500 million postage stamps are issued and sold in this country; which means that, after a suitable reserve has been built up, printing can go steadily along at the rate of 23 millions a day! The printing is performed by contract under the general supervision of officers of the Stores Department.

A special watermarked high-grade paper is used. Paper for each reign has its own special watermark, impressed upon it while it is still wet by "dandy-rolls". For many years past this paper has been supplied by a firm which was manufacturing paper for Bank of England notes a hundred years before there was any thought of postage stamps.

The paper is sent direct from the paper mill to the printing works in the form of 400-lb. rolls in sealed containers. These are all carefully checked, and every piece of paper has eventually to be accounted for, either as sheets, books or rolls of stamps, or as waste. The gum used comes from the Sudan and is the purest gum-arabic obtainable. The ink used in printing is tested frequently for colour and fastness, and is made so that an attempt to remove the cancellation marks from used stamps can be easily detected.

Every step in the various factory processes is carefully scrutinised, and as the sheets come from the machines they are counted and recounted. Some of the printed sheets are made up into books of stamps, or split into rolls for the stamp-selling machines; over 30 million books and 850,000 rolls are turned out every year. If a book or a sheet shows a defect, it is cancelled by black lines printed across the face of the stamps. The slightest sign of mis-printing, variation of colour, marks indicating a flaw in the paper, or the presence of a pin point of oil leads to rejection. Very few imperfect stamps escape the keen eyes of the checkers. Defective impressions and stamps containing errors are most highly prized by the philatelist, but inspection of stamp dealers' catalogues shows that the British Post Office provides them with such varieties only on rare occasions.

The perfect sheets of stamps are counted, checked once more, and made up into parcels of 2,000 sheets each. Finally the packets are sent daily to the stamp section of the Stores Department for issue as required to post offices throughout the country.

CHAPTER 12

FINANCE AND ACCOUNTING

Lord Bridgeman's Committee of 1932 necessarily looms large in any account of the Post Office of to-day; it is perhaps not too much to say that its recommendation for a fundamental alteration in Post Office finance is chiefly responsible for that "new spirit" in the relations between the department and its public which has been, during the past few years, such a marked feature of its development. At the same time it is fair to add that this particular reform had long been advocated within the department and in particular in almost prophetic detail by Sir Evelyn Murray, formerly Secretary to the Post Office, in his book *The Post Office*, published years before the Bridgeman Committee was thought about.

In what one might call pre-Bridgeman days the Exchequer retained, as a matter of course, the whole of the surplus from the working of the Post Office and dealt with it as part of the national income.

Any suggested concessions to the public, therefore, whether in the form of reduction of tariffs or improved facilities, which were materially to affect this surplus would be considered in the light of the immediate financial necessities of the National Budget.

Then came the recommendation that, instead of thus receiving the whole of the excess of receipts over ex-

penditure, "the Exchequer should receive a definite contribution, and that the residue should be made available
for the improvement and development of Post Office
facilities and services to the public". No time was lost
by the Government in accepting this advice and putting
it into practice, and the Finance Act of 1933 made provision on the lines suggested, the contribution from the
Post Office to the Exchequer being fixed initially at
£10,750,000, an amount which was slightly less than the
surplus which the Exchequer received from the earnings
of the Post Office in the financial year 1932–33.

Under these arrangements the "Post Office Net
Surplus" is calculated each year broadly on the basis of
the cash receipts and expenditure of the Post Office, adjusted to take account of services rendered without cash
payment to or by other Government departments. The
amount by which the Post Office Net Surplus exceeds
the fixed Exchequer contribution is paid into the "Post
Office Fund"; if the Net Surplus is less than the contribution the difference is made good to the Exchequer
out of the Post Office Fund.

The effect of the arrangement is, in a real though
somewhat limited sense, to separate the finance of the
Post Office from the national finances, although for
technical reasons its transactions are still included in
the National Budget. When the finances of the Post Office
are sufficiently healthy to provide a surplus over the
liability to the Exchequer, reduced charges for service
and improved facilities can be afforded to the public
without affecting the position of the National Budget.

The Post Office Fund serves in the first place as a
general reserve which can be drawn upon to make up to
the Exchequer its fixed contribution in any year in which,
owing to decline of business, unexpected expenditure or
other contingencies, the surplus for the year should fall
short of the £10,750,000 required for that purpose.

When provision has been made for such reserve as may be thought necessary, the resources of the Post Office Fund are available for the reduction of charges or improvement of services, including capital expenditure on development which otherwise would in ordinary course be met by borrowing. In particular the fund can be used to carry the initial loss arising from concessions to the public which are expected to become self-supporting in due course but which involve a financial sacrifice in the first instance. The net amount in the fund at the end of the financial year 1937–38 was about £3 million.

The institution of this fund has provided the Post Office with new problems of financial administration. Formerly any proposed tariff reduction or expenditure on the improvement of services had to be justified to the Exchequer against the whole field of national requirements. Now it must be judged by its desirability and its cost and then by the fund's resources.

A change which most people would like to see, for instance, is a return to the penny post. If all letters now carried for 1½d. were carried for 1d. the consequent initial loss of revenue would be rather more than £7 million a year. The matter resolves itself therefore into the question whether the Exchequer, with the many claims upon it, can forgo that amount of revenue.

This recent and very progressive development of Post Office policy has not been accompanied by any diminution of the power of control by Parliament over the department's policies and finances. In parliamentary procedure relating to the Post Office there has been no change at all. The Post Office remains a Government department and, as such, conforms to the general rules for the financial administration of the national revenue and expenditure. These rules are based on the principles that (1) the House of Commons shall have complete control over public expenditure and that no Department of State shall incur expenditure which has not previously been sanctioned by Parliament, and (2) the gross produce of all taxes and revenue shall, after certain deductions defined by statute, be paid into one general fund controlled by the Lords Commissioners of the Treasury.

The practical application of these principles means that the Post Office, unlike the ordinary business concern, cannot actually finance its operations out of its revenue. All revenue is in practice paid over to the Exchequer as it is collected and the Exchequer in turn issues to the Post Office the funds required to meet expenditure up to the limits of the amounts voted by Parliament. Prior to 1854 Post Office expenditure, like that of other revenue departments, was paid out of the money it received in the ordinary course of trading with the public, and only the surplus was transferred to the Exchequer. But an Act passed in that year entirely separated revenue from expenditure; henceforth all revenue had to be paid into the Exchequer without deduction and nothing could come out of the Exchequer unless its expenditure was authorised by annual votes of Parliament. This system is still in force.

If, therefore, for any reason Post Office expenditure shows signs of being likely to exceed the amount voted by Parliament, a Supplementary Vote must be obtained to authorise the excess expenditure anticipated, even though additional revenue to an equal or greater amount may be in prospect. As an exception to this rule, the cost of all additional plant and buildings is met from loans from the National Debt Commissioners which are repaid with interest by regular instalments over a fixed period, but the authority of Parliament is required for these loans, and the cost of the annual instalments in repayment form part of the voted expenditure of each year.

The Accounting Officer to the Post Office is responsible to Parliament and to the Treasury for the due collection of revenue and for the accuracy and propriety of all expenditure. The immense scope or the accounting organisation necessary for the proper performance of these duties will be realised in the light of the Post Office activities already described. These activities fall roughly into four categories. First, there are the communication services—the conveyance of letters and parcels, the transmission of telegrams and the provision of the public telephone service, all of which operate locally, nationally and internationally. Secondly, there are services supplementary to these, such as registration and insurance of postal packets, cash on delivery services, express letters, wireless services, private wires, etc. Thirdly, there are the remittance and banking services—money orders, postal orders and Savings Bank; and fourthly, there is a wide range of services performed for other Government departments—the sale of national insurance, income tax, entertainment duty and inland revenue stamps, the issue and repayment of Savings Certificates, the issue of wireless, local taxation and motor licences, the payment of old age and war pensions, etc. In the performance of these services the 24,500 post offices distributed over the country all take their part; the staff of 280,000 employees occupied in the post offices, sorting offices, telephone exchanges or even scattered up and down the roads in gangs, all require to be paid; there are stores and engineering materials to be purchased; road, rail, sea and air conveyance of mails to be paid for; and all the various incidental expenses of the greatest business in the country. The cash passing through the Post Office Accounts in a year amounts to more than £1,500 million, over £950 million of which represents transactions directly with the public.

It is impossible here to give anything like a complete picture of the accounting organisation which has to deal with figures of this magnitude and complexity. Broadly

Mobile post office at a race meeting
Interior, showing storage battery, staff and
telephone cabinet compartments

speaking, the accounting unit is the individual post office on the postal and telegraph side; the District or Area Manager for telephone revenue, and the District Engineer for engineering expenditure of all kinds. On the telephone side the system is in process of change but eventually the unit will be the Telephone Manager, who will be responsible alike for the telephone revenue and the engineering expenditure in his area.

Each accounting unit furnishes a cash account to the Accounting Department at Headquarters, some daily, some weekly and some monthly; these accounts, with their sub-vouchers, form the basis of the accounting system. The number of such accounts dealt with at Headquarters is about 1,700,000 annually, and mechanical processes are as far as possible employed in the work of balancing and summarising the individual items into totals for entry in the ledgers. The accounts are not only checked, but subjected to expert scrutiny with a view to disclosing any manipulation designed to conceal defalcations, and if necessary—though fortunately cases are infrequent—a special check is made of the stocks and accounts of the office in question. The total counter and cash deficiencies, mainly ordinary mistakes and losses, amount to something like 7d. in each £1,000 of transactions with the public.

The cash accounts are also used for the control of cash flowing between the accounting units and the Postmaster-General's account at the Bank of England. Every office remits the whole of its receipts apart from a small balance of till-money and cash required to meet immediately anticipated payments. These remittances are generally made by the smaller sub-offices to their head offices, and by the larger offices to Headquarters by means of cheques on their own public banking accounts with local banks, into which their surplus revenues are paid. It frequently happens however, owing to abnormally large Savings

Bank withdrawals and money order payments, that offices have to pay out more than they receive during the day. To meet these requirements the local banks are used to the fullest possible extent, the procedure being to send a cheque to the head office of the bank, asking it to pay the required amounts to the specified offices. Where banks are not available cash is forwarded from Headquarters. The Cashier's Branch at Headquarters receives remittances amounting to about £132 million and despatches remittances to a value of about £55 million in the course of a year. The Christmas season particularly involves very heavy outward remittances, and during a period of about three weeks just before Christmas the silver which is sent out as part of these remittances weighs about a ton per week.

With a business whose main function is to sell service, a large proportion of Post Office expenditure naturally consists of salary and wages payments, and the annual bill under this heading is over £46 million. Post Office employees fall into a large number of grades, with differing scales of pay, subject to annual increments up to a stipulated maximum; the Post Office is responsible for the assessment and collection of the income tax due from its own employees, and collection is carried out by means of deduction from pay; employees, if they wish, may have life insurance premiums and certain other recognised contributions deducted from their pay in instalments, the department undertaking to hand over the amounts collected to the various companies or societies concerned; and there are at times overtime payments of varying amounts to be made. The preparation of the wages sheets thus becomes a matter of considerable complexity. Moreover, staff is liable to duty throughout the twenty-four hours of the day, while engineering workmen move about from gang to gang and place to place sometimes from day to day; this complicates the process of actual payment.

So far as the international activities of the Post Office are concerned, the necessary accounting arrangements with Empire and foreign countries are laid down either in special agreements or in international conventions, the latter being subject to periodical review at international congresses. These arrangements cover a wide variety of services including the transit of letter and parcel mails, the exchange of money orders and the distribution between the parties concerned of the revenue derived from telephone, telegraph and wireless services. The accounting medium is generally the gold franc. In common with all businesses having foreign relationships, the Post Office international settlements have been complicated by the acute variations in world currencies and by the changes in terms of sterling in the value of the gold franc.

The position of the Post Office as a Government department, with accessible branches all over the country, renders it particularly suitable to undertake the work of making payments to the public involved in social legislation and also for the sale to the public of certain instruments of taxation. The Post Office has in fact been made in some cases, notably those of certain social services, the sole agent for these transactions. Thus the Post Office makes about 223,500,000 pension payments—war pensions, service allowances, old age and widows' pensions—while health and pensions and unemployment insurance stamps are sold to the annual value of over £98 million and about 13 million licences are issued, mainly for wireless and motor cars. The Post Office also sells income tax and entertainment duty stamps. Since these transactions consist mainly of the exchange of paper values for cash, the accounting both between the local and head offices and between the Post Office and the departments concerned is straightforward, though laborious, but it involves frequent settlements with the Government departments concerned.

It has already been explained that the Post Office can only defray expenditure from moneys voted by Parliament. Before therefore any vote can be obtained, an estimate of the expenditure must be presented by the Treasury to the House of Commons. This estimate is classified under a number of sub-heads, each covering a particular type of expenditure such as salaries and wages, conveyance of mails, engineering materials, superannuation. Its compilation is a matter which requires meticulous care, and although the Post Office financial year begins on April 1 the detailed preparation of the estimate begins in the previous autumn.

The heads of all departments are first asked to furnish particulars of their anticipated expenditure under the various sub-heads. Under the new regional organisation, which will be described later, each region will also prepare its own budget, comprising the requirements of its Head Postmasters and Telephone Managers as well as its own headquarters expenditure. These local budgets will then be embodied with those of the Headquarters departments and the whole will form the basis of the complete Post Office budget.

When the estimates are finally compiled and approved by the Postmaster-General, they are forwarded to the Treasury with full explanatory notes, which incidentally cover any variations from the estimates of the previous year.

The Treasury closely scrutinises the estimates before presentation and from time to time they are examined in detail by an Estimates Committee of the House of Commons.

The next stage is that prior to April 1, in each year, the House votes a sum of money by a "Vote on Account" to carry on the service until the estimate has been finally approved. Later in the session, the estimate comes before the Committee of Supply for approval. Finally, in Committee of Ways and Means, money is voted to make good the supply granted and the money is appropriated to the particular service by an Appropriation Act.

The heads of Headquarters departments and other responsible officers are advised by the Comptroller and Accountant General early in the year of the amounts under each sub-head which have been allotted to them, and they are expected to keep their expenditure within those amounts. All expenditure is, of course, recorded and brought to account under its appropriate sub-head of the vote and at the end of the year an appropriation account is drawn up and presented to Parliament showing the actual expenditure over the year under the several sub-heads, an explanation being given of any material divergence from the provision in the estimate.

The Post Office, like any other great trading concern, must ascertain and demonstrate to its shareholders (in this case the whole public) the financial results of its trading. These results are not obtainable from the parliamentary accounts already described, which are purely cash statements, and many complex adjustments are necessary before a true trading account for the year can be compiled. For example, the value of postal work and agency services rendered without payment to other Government departments, the expenditure of other departments such as the Stationery Office and the Office of Works incurred on behalf of the Post Office, must be taken into account. Figures must also be adjusted to an income and expenditure basis. In a number of other important respects also the cash accounts with the

Exchequer fail to reflect adequately the true financial results of the operation of the Post Office services.

There is the further complication that the Post Office is carrying on three different types of business, postal, telegraph and telephone, and administration can only be effective if the results of these activities are known separately. The difficulties of separating them are enhanced by the fact that the Post Office is operated as a closely interlocking organisation, as will be realised from a consideration of the duties of, say, a counter clerk who in the course of a day's duty may sell postage stamps, accept telegrams, receive payment of telephone accounts, transact Savings Bank business, pay old age pensions and perform many other diverse services. In practice various accounting and statistical devices are employed for obtaining all the information necessary for an accurate analysis of the expenditure on these services; these are not of general interest, though of profound interest to the accountant and administrator.

Separate profit and loss accounts on a strictly commercial model are therefore prepared and presented to Parliament each year. The accounts are published annually by the Stationery Office under the title of the *Post Office Commercial Accounts*.

It will be understood from what has been said that the department under the control of the Comptroller and Accountant General, who is responsible for all Post Office accounting arrangements and for examining and reporting upon the financial aspects of all proposals having monetary implications, is not the least of the Headquarters departments either in importance or size. Actually it employs a clerical staff of about 1,500, of whom rather less than half are women. It was early realised that much of the work was of a character that, even in Victorian days, could be regarded as suitable for women. The department was accordingly one of the pioneers in this field, and the experiment was of course speedily and completely justified.

Even if it were otherwise, it is doubtful whether anyone in these days would be so rash or ungallant to report as did the Secretary of the Post Office to the Postmaster-General in 1872. After one year's experience of the employment of women in the Accountant General's Department on checking stamps on telegrams to ensure that the correct amount had been paid, he reported: "The work, which consists entirely of fault-finding, is well within the capacity of women and has been satisfactorily performed."

CHAPTER 13

ORGANISATION AND CONTROL

It is time to glance at the controls of this great machine and to get an idea of the general organisation of the Post Office.

It is in one sense an inconvenient moment to do so and yet, at the same time, a most interesting one, because the whole organisation of the Post Office is at present being re-formed.

The public attitude towards State organisations generally has since the War undergone a big change. A State trading department has been in the past regarded with some suspicion, which did not necessarily tend to diminish as the trading grew in prosperity. But this feeling had gone by the 'twenties. There were fewer misgivings about State enterprise and there grew up a public opinion that a trading department owned by the public might be, indeed *should* be, expected to aim at a standard of efficiency at least as high as that of a business owned privately.

Suspicious eyes were directed at the Post Office to see if it satisfied this test and eventually a demand arose for an inquiry. The Government complied with the demand by appointing a committee consisting of Lord Bridgeman, Lord Plender and Lord (then Sir John) Cadman. Their report, presented to the Postmaster-General, Sir Kingsley

Wood, after a very rapid investigation, found that the criticisms levied at the Post Office were in the main not well founded. To many Post Office services and departments they paid handsome tribute—in particular to the technical progress made of recent years in the telephone service. Indeed they expressed their opinion that on the whole the Post Office did its job with remarkable efficiency.

The committee did, however, draw attention to what seemed to them to be defects in the organisation which called for remedy, especially an over-centralisation of direction and responsibility at Headquarters. They also found fault with the practice under which all the Post Office profits went as a matter of course into the Treasury. They rejected a proposal which had been made to remove the Post Office from the control of a Postmaster-General and, incidentally, from the control of Parliament. They rejected also the proposal that the telephone service should be divorced from the Post Office and set up in an establishment of its own. They expressed the view that telegraphs and telephones were so closely interlinked and the two together, especially telegraphs, so interwoven with the mail service, both as regards buildings, staff and common plant, that separation was indeed not a practical question. Rather than revolution and disintegration they advocated measures of reorganisation and adaptation, accompanied by a fundamental change in Post Office finance which has already been dealt with in its appropriate place.

By way of administrative changes the committee suggested, first, the establishment of a board to consider and construct policy, with the Postmaster-General as its chairman, a Director General, the permanent head of the service, as its deputy chairman (actually the Assistant Postmaster-General, who is a Member of Parliament, acts as joint deputy chairman), and a Deputy Director

General and the heads of the various departments as its members. Secondly, to execute the policy arrived at by this board, the committee recommended the division of the country into a number of regions, each under a Regional Director, upon whom a large measure of responsibility would be devolved.

The Government accepted the report and a quick beginning was made in carrying out its recommendations. The Post Office Board was set up; Colonel Donald Banks (later Sir Donald Banks, K.C.B.) was appointed the first Director General, with Mr Thomas Gardiner (now Sir Thomas Gardiner, K.C.B., K.B.E.) as his deputy. At the time of their appointment Colonel Banks was Controller of the Post Office Savings Bank and Mr Gardiner Controller of the London Postal Service; Sir Thomas Gardiner succeeded to the post of Director General when, in 1936, Sir Donald Banks was appointed Secretary to the Air Ministry. Quite recently the supreme control has been strengthened by the appointment of an Assistant Director General.

The Director General is responsible for action following upon the conclusions of the board, and for the general direction of the Post Office services. He deals also with savings, engineering and legal matters and with general finance. The Deputy Director General, while acting generally as deputy in all matters, deals particularly with questions of service, whether postal, telegraph or telephone. The Assistant Director General's particular responsibility is for personnel and buildings, and for public relations.

In addition to the Postmaster-General, the Assistant Postmaster-General, the Director General and his Deputy and Assistant, the Post Office Board at present comprises the Engineer-in-Chief, the Comptroller and Accountant General, the Director of Telecommunications, the Director of Postal Services, the Director of Savings, the

Public Relations Officer and the Regional Director for Scotland.

The Headquarters administration as now constituted comprises three main departments: Postal Services, Tele-communications, and Personnel. These are supplemented by seven other departments: the Accountant General's, Engineering, Money Order, Public Relations, Savings Bank, Solicitor's and Stores Departments. The administrative departments are responsible for the direction of policy and co-ordination, and the allied departments co-operate with them.

While the reconstitution of the supreme control to the pattern described was put in hand as soon as possible after the Bridgeman Committee had reported, the main change in administration which it recommended, the division of the country into more or less autonomous regions, was taken in hand very cautiously and has indeed only just emerged from the experimental stage. Since this process constitutes one of the greatest administrative developments ever carried out in this country, either in private business or public administration, it is worthy of some description.

Hitherto the control centralised in London had been exercised through various channels, more or less independent of each other. London had its own postal service presided over by a Controller, its own telephone service and its Central Telegraph Office. Outside London, postal and telegraph control was in the hands of 13 Surveyors, and 9 Postmaster-Surveyors who ruled over the 9 largest towns. Telephones were controlled on the commercial side by 26 District Managers and on the engineering side by 14 Superintending Engineers, all having a separate line of communication to London.

To convert this fan-shaped contrivance into the pattern set by the Bridgeman Committee without disturbing the even flow of business, which increases in a spectacular degree almost from day to day, was obviously a matter of some delicacy. It was tackled by a departmental committee under Sir Thomas Gardiner, whose first task was to ascertain the lowest level to which devolution could be carried compatible with efficiency, then to provide the widest possible means of co-ordination at every stage in the organisation, and to ensure smooth working of the various Post Office services where two or more of them are concerned together.

As soon as preliminary studies were completed, two provincial regions were set up; this was in March 1936. One consisted of the whole of Scotland with its headquarters at Edinburgh, the other comprised North-East England with headquarters at Leeds. Later the same year London became a region, or rather two regions—a postal region and a telegraph and telephone region. Thus yet another London comes into being, a London covering for postal purposes an area of 234 square miles. Other regions will come into existence gradually: a North-Western Region with headquarters at Manchester, a Midland with headquarters at Birmingham, a South-Western centred on Bristol, a "Wales and Border Counties" with headquarters at Cardiff, a Home Counties Region and a Northern Ireland Region. As each of these new machines runs itself into working order, it is being watched unceasingly for particles of grit, for any sort of friction or functional awkwardness, so that mistakes can be remedied as the mechanisation proceeds and every lubricant applied that makes for easy working.

From the telephone point of view the outstanding feature of the reorganisation is the division of the country into 46 telephone areas in which the responsibilities for traffic and engineering, hitherto divided between the District Manager and the Superintending Engineer, are unified under a single control. Thus the Scottish Region contains five areas and the North-Eastern Region seven, each under its "Telephone Manager" who owes allegiance, of course, to the Regional Director.

This particular feature of the new plan is being developed in advance of the creation of new regions, a policy which will not only obviate delay in bringing telephone administration into line with the requirements of a rapidly growing service, but also facilitates the setting up of the regions themselves.

As the regional organisation stands at present, each Regional Director has a board, corresponding somewhat in form to the Headquarters Board. It consists of the Deputy Regional Director and five functional experts: Postal Controller, Telecommunications Controller, Chief Regional Engineer, Staff Controller and Regional Finance Officer; each of these experts has with him at regional headquarters the assistants necessary for the carrying out of his functions. Taking the Scottish Region as an example, many of the questions formerly referred along ten lines of communication to London will be settled at Edinburgh; the residue will be transmitted along one channel only, that controlled by the Regional Director who, before sending a proposal up to Headquarters, will co-ordinate all aspects of it affecting Scotland as a whole.

The same principle will be extended to other regions as they are formed, and it is hoped that the result of the change will be to make all the services of the Post Office more quickly responsive and more readily adaptable to local needs and developments, while at the same time limiting the functions of Headquarters in London in a large measure to the framing of policy, the regulation of rates and general co-ordination of services.

The Regional Director and his Deputy will, as a rule, be complementary to each other; that is to say, if the Director's previous experience has been mainly postal, the Deputy will generally be drawn from the engineering or telephone spheres, and *vice versa*—thus giving effect to the Bridgeman Committee's recommendation that engineering and technical staff should have access to the highest administrative posts. The important point, however, is that the Regional Director is responsible for all branches of Post Office work in his region.

One of the results of the new organisation is the abolition of the old Surveying Corps which came into existence early.in the reign of George I for the purpose of safeguarding the royal monopoly in the carriage of letters. The Surveying Branch grew in importance till it became responsible for a great part of provincial administration. Its annals are particularly picturesque and it is to be hoped that, before the last surveyor disappears with the completion of regionalisation, the Corps will have found its own historian to do justice to its achievements and traditions.

Anthony Trollope was a surveyor, until at the age of 52 he determined that the time had come to give undivided allegiance to novel writing. He was contemporary with Rowland Hill and had no love for the great reformer. "It was a pleasure to me to differ from him on all occasions," he records, "and looking back now, I think that in all such differences I was right." Which comment well illustrates Trollope's general attitude. Incidentally, both Hill and Trollope in their respective autobiographies claim to have originated pillar boxes, but as Rowland Hill dates their introduction to 1840, at which time Trollope was still living a "wretched life" as a clerk in the London General Post Office, Hill's claim must be given preference.

In gauging the magnitude of the reorganisation which has been described it should be realised that to-day the Post Office, with over 280,000 employees, is the largest employer in the country, though it is only recently that it reached this position by forging slightly ahead of the London, Midland and Scottish Railway. The diversity of its services naturally involves the employment of many grades and types. First of all, in the Headquarters departments both in London and the provinces there is not only a large administrative and clerical establishment, but also a considerable professional, technical and specialist staff, including engineers, solicitors, architects, and doctors.

The largest group of all is the manipulative staff: postmen, sorting clerks and telegraphists, counter clerks, telephonists and messengers, each grade with its due allowance of higher posts—supervisors, superintendents or inspectors.

Head Postmasters, of whom there are about 450, are originally appointed mainly from the ranks of supervising officers; if they prove successful, they may be promoted to larger offices. All vacancies are advertised in the *Post Office Circular* and applications are invited. At one time a son often succeeded his father in a postmastership—the Dover office was held by one family, named Norwood, for over a century—but family claims ceased to have weight about the end of last century. A Head Postmaster's control extends not only to the town in which the head office is situated but also to the area around that town, frequently a very wide one. The whole country outside Inner London is in fact covered by the 450 Head Post Office Districts.

There are two kinds of sub-offices. The larger offices, generally speaking, known as salaried sub-offices, are in charge of postmasters and are staffed by permanent pensionable Post Office personnel. There are about 700 of these. The other kind of offices—known officially as scale payment sub-offices—some 23,000 in number, deserve special mention. The sub-postmasters or subpostmistresses—for a large proportion of sub-offices are in the hands of women—are in effect contractors. They are remunerated by a "scale payment" based on the volume of work they perform—the sales over the counter, the mails received and despatched, the amount of telephone work, etc.—and so long as the work is performed satisfactorily and adequate accommodation is provided the authorities do not mind whether the sub-postmaster does the work himself or delegates it to a competent substitute, be it a member of his family or a paid assistant. Usually the Post Office work in villages and suburbs is carried on in connection with some other business, of which the general store and grocery shop is the most common.

The management of the sub-offices under his control gives a Head Postmaster a variety of problems and often a variety of entertainment. An analysis of one Head Postmaster's district in the North shows that of 176 scale payment sub-offices 66 are held by grocers or general storekeepers. Other occupations cover a wide range from that of stationer or confectioner (these two account for 27 between them) to antique dealer, abbey custodian and "fish-and-chips fryer".

Among sub-postmasters there are degrees of sophistication and character as wide apart as those of occupation. There is one elderly sub-postmistress in this north country district who firmly refuses to have the telephone installed because she is "frit on 'em". Another, over 90 years of age, reported that she had relegated her Post Office duties to her son and daughter (72 and 70 respectively) because she found she had quite enough to do in the garden! And an octogenarian sub-postmaster replies to the Head Postmaster's kindly enquiry after his health by announcing that he has just bought a new bike on the hire-purchase system!

The younger generation may not supply so much of the

humour but all alike supply fine service to the community, and it will be obvious that without a system such as that under which the country sub-postmaster works, the cost of supplying the full facilities of the Post Office to a small isolated village would, as a rule, be prohibitive.

For the conduct of its business throughout the country the Post Office occupies a very large number of properties—some 6,000 in all: post offices, telephone exchanges, engineering shops, stores depots, factories and garages. St Martin's-le-Grand itself, the Headquarters of all this activity, is on a site acquired in 1815 and formerly occupied by an old monastery which housed the secular clergy who served the Cathedral Church of St Paul; this original St Martin's possessed the right of Sanctuary. It may be said that so rapid has been the growth of the Post Office that, in spite of many changes and additions, the Headquarters buildings have never, since the first St Martin's-le-Grand was opened in 1829, proved sufficient for current requirements. The most notable addition of the present century was the King Edward Building, on the site of the original Christ's Hospital; King Edward VII laid the foundation stone of this fine building in 1905.

The most notable achievement of the Post Office, speaking architecturally, has, however, been the progressive modernisation of all Crown offices which has been taking place since 1929 and is now practically completed. One can recall the time when post offices were somewhat drab and dingy, often cluttered up with all manner of untidy notices. The economy measures that followed the War were in part responsible for this state of affairs; building costs had to be kept at the lowest possible level consistent with the maintenance of the public services.

Nowadays the Post Office compares with the most modern of banks; it is light and well fitted, public notices are kept within strict bounds, garish commercial advertisements which defaced the walls have given place to pleasant and instructive posters illustrating Post Office services, there are in the larger offices chairs to sit on if one wants to write a note; in fact the "brighter Post Office" campaign has well justified its name.

The improvement in the public offices has been accompanied by a corresponding reconditioning of the parts of the office which the public does not ordinarily see. Special attention has been given to the well-being of the staff; working conditions and equipment have been improved very materially, retiring rooms tastefully and comfortably furnished, cooking arrangements modernised, and, in short, staff comfort is studied in its proper relation to efficient public service.

The provision of Post Office buildings is never finished. The business grows so rapidly that the problem of housing it is never solved. Between one and two millions a year has been the common measure of building expenditure during the past few years. A staff of architects both at G.P.O. Headquarters and at the Office of Works are kept busy devising new plans, incorporating every practical modern improvement—and always giving employment.

Post Office business is not, however, entirely conducted in solid buildings of brick or stone. Winding its way down a lane on the way to a country show or sports meeting one may nowadays meet one of the new Mobile Post Offices. There are two of them, registered by special permission of the Ministry of Transport as "GPO 1" and "GPO 2". They represent the latest sign of the desire of the authorities to put themselves in the same relation to the public as Mahomet adopted towards the Mountain. They consist of a tractor and a trailer, constructed to negotiate the most awkward twisting lanes and narrow gateways, and the distinctive red colouring of the Mobile Post Office is quite sufficient advertisement of its presence; how the bulls regard it when it goes to cattle shows one trembles to think.

The body of the vehicle is in three compartments—the Post Office proper, accommodation for sound-proof telephone cabinets, and a store-room. When the Mobile Post Office reaches its destination an awning is extended as a protection from sun and wind, and duckboards are put down to keep the customers' feet dry; the window is thrown open, the telephone line is connected up by aerial cable, the clerks take their seats and ordinary business, including the despatch and receipt of telegrams and telephone calls to the most remote parts of the country, proceeds as normally as in any other Post Office. No one will ever be able to say again that the Post Office stands still.

The principal functions and activities of the main departments of the Post Office have been described, or at least outlined, in previous chapters, but in dealing specially with Headquarters there are one or two ancillary services which should not pass unnoticed.

First there is the Medical Service. It was in 1855 that a whole time medical officer was first appointed to "examine all candidates for appointment, to inquire into cases in which there is suspicion of feigned or exaggerated illness; to give advice and administer medicine at the General Post Office to all the officers of whatever grade who are attached to this office or to the Money Order Office; to attend at their own houses such of these officers as belong to the class of Letter Carriers, Stampers, Porters, Messengers, etc., and as reside within four miles of the General Post Office and who are unable to leave home; to examine from time to time into the Sanitary conditions of the Chief Office and its branches; to examine applicants for pension with a view to its being ascertained whether the state of their health is such as to render their retirement necessary; to afford medical aid and in any other way the Postmaster-General thinks it is right to direct."

This formula reads quaintly to-day, 83 years later, when the Medical Service comprises, in addition to a Head-quarters staff of 11, some 2,600 local medical officers distributed over the whole country.

The Headquarters medical officers give clinical atten-tion to the large central staff of men and women in London; on an average they see 70,000 patients every year and examine some 5,000 candidates for entrance into the service.

But apart from performing these normal functions the Medical Department of the Post Office has the dis-tinction of being probably the largest industrial medical service in the world, and it has been able to accumulate complete sick records, under actual working conditions, of nearly a quarter of a million men and women between 16 and 60 years of age.

These records have proved useful in several ways. They have recently provided a particularly interesting comparison. An unselected consecutive series of 200 London boys of 16, seeking employment in the Post Office, coming from the same sorts of families and living in similar districts, was compared with a similar series of 200 London boys of the same years who had been examined 25 years previously. The present-day boys were found to weigh on an average 16 lb. a boy more, and to be 1½ inches taller, than those of the previous generation. A similar comparison between similar groups of 200 girls of 16 showed that the girls of to-day weighed on an average 9 lb. a girl more, and were 1 inch taller, than the girls of the last generation.

This was an investigation that could probably have

been made in no other industry, and there is no doubt that the records contain still unworked mines of valuable information both for industry and medicine, information of a kind which even the most efficient "follow-up" departments of hospitals could scarcely obtain.

Another department which comes into the public eye very little, and then generally only in connection with the criminal side of its work, is the Solicitor's.

The Post Office has employed its own legal adviser for a very long time—certainly for over 235 years. The earliest record dates from the year 1702 and, with the exception of a brief period of seven years between 1714 and 1721, the list of persons holding the office is complete.

During this period there have been only 14 Solicitors, which suggests that the tenure of a solicitor has been a relatively good risk compared with that of a Postmaster-General or even of a Secretary or Director General. There have been 87 Postmasters-General and 22 Secretaries or Directors General during the same period.

Prior to the year 1838 the Solicitor received a small salary and was paid ordinary professional fees for all the work which he did for the Post Office, except for the advice given. In that year he was incorporated into the establishment and has since remained a permanent official. His officers are also now established.

There is a "Solicitor to the Post Office in Scotland" who has a separate responsibility. But the conduct of all legal work in the rest of the United Kingdom rests with the Solicitor at Headquarters, whose department consists of 26 professionally qualified officers (either barristers or solicitors) with the necessary non-professional and clerical staff.

The Solicitor acts for all the Headquarters departments and—except of course in Scotland—he will also act for the Regional Directors. He advises the departments on all legal questions which arise and deals with civil and criminal work, parliamentary and conveyancing work and litigation in all courts.

The criminal work entails the prosecution of all offenders against the Post Office, whether employed by the department or members of the general public. A large proportion of the prosecutions come under the Wireless Telegraphy Acts.

On the other hand, in suitable cases the Solicitor also undertakes the defence of officers of the Post Office against whom proceedings, either civil or criminal, are taken in respect of acts alleged to have been committed in the course of their duty. For instance, since the Road Traffic Acts created a multitude of new offences, a few drivers of Post Office motor vehicles have been defended against charges made against them, and officers are similarly defended against charges of negligence, and even of libel and slander.

Apart from these cases in which the individual is concerned, many matters of outstanding importance are dealt with in the Solicitor's Department. The transfer of the National Telephone Company's undertaking to the State in 1912 and the arbitration which followed, and in more recent years the transfer of the transatlantic cables and wireless stations to Imperial and International Communication Company, Ltd. (now Cable and Wireless, Ltd.), are merely examples of the important and diverse matters which demand attention. And in addition there is the continuous preparation of contracts involving the expenditure of millions of pounds of public money.

Lastly, there is the Public Relations Department, set up a few years ago by Sir Kingsley Wood, then Postmaster-General. "Public Relations" is an American name for an administrative activity which is comparatively new in this country, and the Post Office was, at all events in the sphere of Government, a pioneer in its adoption.

The Post Office was well suited to this role. It was a great business as well as a Government department. It had things to sell—services, which are much more intangible and mysterious than commodities. It had been subjected to a considerable body of criticism, much of which, as the Bridgeman Committee reported, was "uninformed and irresponsible", while some no doubt was "genuine and thoughtful, coming from authoritative and disinterested sources".

The function of the new department was, briefly, to "project" and explain the numerous, and constantly growing, activities of the Post Office. The first Public Relations Officer, Sir Stephen Tallents, brought with him wide experience in the methods of persuasion gained as Secretary of the Empire Marketing Board. He elaborated and extended the existing publicity arrangements, so that very quickly the public came to a more complete understanding and appreciation of all that the Post Office meant to them. The result was a growing feeling of confidence and goodwill and a growing inclination to co-operate. In this atmosphere the Post Office to-day goes vigorously ahead.

The Public Relations Department works through a variety of channels. It is the task of one division to keep the Press fully informed on all developments and to be always ready to assist in the collection of any information that may be required. The Press, on its side, gives invaluable assistance to the Postmaster-General in such matters as the "Post Early" campaign. This happy co-operation extends to the provinces. Each region, as it is formed, has its own Regional Public Relations Officer, so that while the efforts of Headquarters are relayed and amplified, attention is also given to local needs in the matter of publicity.

The close relations with Chambers of Commerce and Trade, which have existed for many years, have been encouraged and extended. Sometimes this connection is formed through the medium of special local advisory committees, more often by direct contact between the Chairman or Secretary of the Chamber and the local Head Postmaster. When some big change of practice is contemplated, business interests are taken into council at Headquarters and consulted about methods and re-actions. This sort of co-operation has been most fruitful. Over and above this the Postmaster-General has his Advisory Council which meets periodically and reviews Post Office plans and progress.

In many other ways the Post Office now makes itself known to its customers: by its posters and booklets, its newspaper advertisements and leaflets, by the work of its own film unit, its exhibitions and shops and, by no means least, its work in the schools of the country. With the cordial co-operation of educational authorities 28,000 schools up and down the country receive periodically sets of posters with explanatory literature. Many schools, too, are visited by travelling film projection units, and by this means some half a million children yearly have the various services of the Post Office interpreted to them.

The G.P.O. films reach further large audiences, both adult and juvenile, throughout the country through a special film library which is managed, in connection with the Empire Film Library, by the Director of the Imperial Institute. This happy association of the two libraries gives the Post Office films access to all those schools, churches, societies and clubs which have their own projectors; the number of these is steadily growing. At present the films are seen by over 2 million people every year. Every opportunity is taken of showing them to the staff to feed and stimulate their interest in the general working of the machine of which they form part. This is an essential part

Post Office posters: above, from a school set by John Vickery; below, "Motor Transport Workshop" by Lili Réthi

of a public relations policy. With the same object the various sections of the work are described in publications known as *Green Papers* and a staff magazine is published which has a circulation of 180,000.

Major G. C. Tryon, during his Postmaster-Generalship, has given immense stimulus to the public relations policy inaugurated by his predecessor. He has personally taken a leading part in the projection of his great department into the public mind, and with his active encouragement the Post Office has built up an effective instrument for interpretation and persuasion. This instrument has helped to produce public appreciation of, and indeed pride in, Post Office services, and has helped moreover to a quick understanding of the difficulties which have occasionally to be met in giving the public exactly what it wants.

Such difficulties are passing phases in the life of a great department. The Post Office of to-day not only makes its mighty contribution to the life of the nation, and of the Empire, with an efficiency which is universally admitted and admired; it is also well equipped to grasp every opportunity which the science of communications may offer for the purpose of improving its services and keeping itself abreast of the times.

INDEX